Expecting the Unexpected

An Honest Look at Miscarriage, Postpartum Depression & Motherhood

Amy Kim

Expecting the Unexpected:
An Honest Look at Miscarriage, Postpartum Depression &
Motherhood

ISBN 10: 0-9898418-2-0
ISBN 13: 978-0-9898418-2-5

The inclusion of an internet link or specific brand is not intended as an endorsement of any product, service, or advertisement and the author does not guarantee the accuracy of content found at any website link.

The purpose of this book is to educate and inform. For medical advice you should seek the individual, personal services of a medical professional.

Library of Congress Control Number: 2015931329

Cover designed by Amy Byon
Amy Byon is a freelance artist and studied Fashion Design at Parsons the New School for Design, earning a bachelor's degree in Fine Arts. She was born and raised in New York, and currently resides in Southern California with her husband, Tae, and her two boys, Luke and Jude. You can learn more about Amy on her blog at www.jotpot.blogspot.com.

Published by Eurydice Press
www.eurydicepress.com

For Kevin, who gave me the courage to write.

For Aliya, who gave me the words to write.

For KJ, who has filled my heart with even more love than I ever thought possible.

CONTENTS

INTRODUCTION

Grief has a way of either isolating individuals or bringing them together.

After my miscarriage and experience with postpartum depression, I was not at all prepared for the waves of grief and despair that followed. There were many days when I thought I would never feel better. And I began searching just about everywhere to see if there were others like me. I was searching for hope, for some sort of good news that things would get better.

I began writing as an exercise in breathing and living again. Shared stories and experiences have a unique way of connecting us to one another and reminding us we are not alone. I wrote these essays not only as a way to heal, but also with the hope that others might find some comfort in knowing someone else had a rough start to motherhood, and was made all the better for it.

SUNFLOWERS

I've never really been the type of girl who loves flowers. In fact, when Kevin and I started dating I told him from the get go, "No flowers necessary." You might be surprised to learn it really is possible to kill a dozen beautiful flowers within three days. I was a champion flower killer back in those days.

Something changed a few years into our marriage. I began to linger in the floral section of local grocery stores. Every now and then I would pick up a gorgeous arrangement, usually something bright with a wide array of colors, and say to Kevin, "Aren't these pretty?" And then they would come home to live with us and I would manage to keep them alive for four or five days. This was surely a sign of growth. While they were not frequent guests in our home, I began looking forward to having them over for more than special occasions.

A couple of months ago we were on a trek back home from vacation with a couple of our friends. As we were munching on sunflower seeds I asked (out loud unfortunately), "Where do sunflower seeds come from?" After about 30 seconds of complete silence, Kevin reluctantly answered first: **SUNFLOWERS**. Of course. I am not sure how long we all laughed, but I do remember it was the kind of laughing that makes you grab your stomach because it hurts so much after it is all over.

A heart-breaking journey began for me that very night. After an ultrasound, multiple blood tests, and an endless amount of waiting, on August 23, just five days before what was supposed to be my first prenatal appointment, I received confirmation I had miscarried. It was just the beginning of what would be days, weeks, and months of tears, and more tears. On the day of the ultrasound, upon learning there was no baby or heartbeat to be found, I felt like I had died.

I remember everything from that day. I remember I was wearing a lavender top, shorts, and flip flops. I remember the exact time I called the doctor's office. I remember I was supposed to give a presentation at work and I felt extremely guilty having to call in sick. I remember Kevin stopped to get a disgusting croissant breakfast sandwich on our way to the Emergency Room. I remember I had to drink so much water before the ultrasound I thought I would wet my pants. I remember the hospital felt particularly cold that day and everyone in it looked absolutely miserable. I remember thinking all of this couldn't possibly be happening and all I wanted to do was to wake up from this nightmare. I remember I couldn't do anything that day. I remember being a zombie and I had cried so hard, even getting up to go to the bathroom required tremendous effort. I remember thinking I should feed my husband and wondering what we would eat for dinner. I remember Kevin leaving to go get groceries for dinner and bringing home just what I needed – **a beautiful bouquet of bright yellow sunflowers**.

I remember laughing when I saw the sunflowers in his hand. I was in so much pain, I didn't think it was possible, but I laughed hard. I remember staring into the center of the flower, skeptical and wondering, "Do sunflower seeds really come from sunflowers?" I remember staring at those sunflowers up and down and sideways and hopping onto the internet to find out just exactly how these bad boys were made. And so for that week, every time I passed by the kitchen table and looked at my sunflowers, I smiled. I smiled because of my husband, who knows just the thing to make me smile when I am absolutely wrecked. I smiled because for six weeks, I was blessed to carry our baby. I smiled because I was reminded of all of the love and the amazing friends we have in our lives, without whom I am sure I would have fallen apart. I smiled for all of these reminders – even in the midst of chaos, I was definitely not alone.

LIGHT in the midst of DARKNESS

HOPE in the midst of PAIN

JOY in the midst of SORROW

For all of these reminders and more, I am thankful for my sunflowers.

"TODAY I WILL NOT SHOULD ON MYSELF"

I first heard this line from the late Brennan Manning during a talk he gave years ago, and thought it was brilliant. As I have been sharing with more and more people about my miscarriage, I have been mulling over what this means. Many people, well-meaning and loving people, will respond to a miscarriage in a number of ways. Here are some things I have heard one too many times:

- You're young and healthy! You'll get pregnant again.

- It will happen. Don't worry.

- Miscarriage is very common.

- My [fill in the blank] had multiple miscarriages and now she has healthy kids and is expecting one on the way!

- Something must have been defective with the baby, and maybe your body is just doing what it's supposed to do.

Others will ask you a hundred and one questions, none of which you have answers for of course. Why did this happen? Did you do anything to cause it? Will it happen again? Will you start trying again? Are you worried? Why are you crying? Is something wrong? I have a clever and snarky response to all of these and maybe one day I will share them with you. It would be absolutely wonderful if there were always an explanation for the painful events in our lives and the subsequent grief.

And one of the most aggravating responses begins with this phrase: "You should ..." You should pray and read Scripture. You should go somewhere safe and quiet and really cry out to God. You should ask God what he wants you to learn from all of this. You should know that God loves you and has a plan for you. You should trust God.

And I probably should.

But all I want to do when I hear those words is rip my ears off and throw them at the person who had enough gall and stupidity to say them. I remember a few months after my one of my close friends had miscarried, she shared some concerns with me about having to attend an upcoming bachelorette party where horseback riding and wine tasting were just some of the items on the agenda. I remember stupidly responding by saying, "You should go! Babies are resilient; you should not feel like you have to put your life on hold every month. You should go, relax, and have fun with your girls. You deserve it." I count three "shoulds" in that response. What I deserved was a punch to the face, but my friend was gracious enough to let it go.

I failed to understand my friend was still intensely grieving the loss of her baby. I had forgotten this conversation was taking place just a few weeks after her baby would have been born had she carried the baby to full-term. I did not realize how instead of feeling celebratory about her friend's upcoming nuptials, she was carefully considering how she could best prepare her body in the very event a baby just might be growing in her womb after endless months of waiting, hoping, and longing.

I had no idea.

All I could think in the moment was I wanted my friend to be happy again. And so I think friends and loved ones do this – they share their platitudes and try to say something or relate in whatever way they can, hoping to make you feel better in the process, but most of the time you are left feeling worse, not better, and even more alone in your pain.

I am just beginning to learn grieving is a long and arduous process. Some of the most comforting moments these last few months have been when people were simply present with me. They sat with me, listened to me, and mourned with me. I imagine this is what sitting Shiva looks like. Others would remind me that they were thinking of me and continuously praying for Kevin and me. These moments helped me to be honest when all I wanted to do was run and hide.

So for today, I will not should on myself. I am certain there are a million things I should be doing, but for now I will write and just be.

RAIN

WRITTEN AFTER MY MISCARRIAGE IN OCTOBER 2010

Today I wanted it to rain. And I **hate** the rain.

I hate the rain for hundreds of different reasons. For starters, the first and only time I got into a major car accident was on a day of "first rain" (if you live in Southern California where we never experience any kind of weather, you will understand what this means). I suppose the combination of slick roads and my balding tires is what might have caused this. To say this was a near-death experience may verge on the side of being dramatic, but I did black out upon impact and came out with a pretty badly bruised face. In any event, my war wounds made me look bad ass.

Other reasons: Worms. Gross. I was walking Kobe (my dog) the other day and must have kicked or splashed one up onto my bare leg. This resulted in screams and subsequent shivers once I got indoors.

Did I also mention that I wear glasses? Wiping them in the rain doesn't help either. Try looking through water-streaked glasses for a few hours and you will want to rip your eyeballs out. I suppose the alternative would be to not wear them and bump into things.

And of course there are hundreds of other reasons.

I think I may be in the minority when I say I hate the rain. Most people I know can't wait for the rainy season. They love to sit by the fireplace and curl up with a good book or play the piano while they hear the pitter patter outside. Not me. I prefer sunny skies to a downpour.

But today, I welcomed the rain.

I have been reading a book titled *Bittersweet* by Shauna Niequist. Have you ever read a book that so perfectly described all of the thoughts and emotions swirling around in your head, some you didn't even know you had or, at the very least, didn't have the capacity to express in the moment? This book has been a pure gift, but it has also made my heart raw and exposed.

Surely people deal with pain and grief in a variety of ways. Some may self-medicate with drugs or happy juice. Others might eat their hearts out, filling themselves with anything and everything until their guts are ready to explode. Or if you're like me, you will keep yourself busy to the point of no return. Pile on the work, dinners with girlfriends, date nights, movies, and in the quiet moments do everything in your power to occupy your time with mind-numbing cell phone games. Or you might even exercise and beat the hell out of your body just so you can crash when the rest of the world is sleeping. You do anything you can do to keep your mind running ... just keep moving.

And then there are others who might shave their heads like they did in biblical times. I'm certainly not gutsy or adorable enough for that. Try imagining me with a shaved head and thick glasses. Just slap some pearl earrings on me and call me Mrs. Potato Head.

Today I welcomed the rain.

THE FUNNY THING IS

OCTOBER 28, 2010

The idea of having children of my own has long since sent chills up and down my spine.

While I have always adored babies – I'm usually the one snuggling with a baby in the corner – the idea of being responsible for nurturing and growing another human being has been absolutely terrifying.

Labor and delivery had not scared me much until my nephew was born this past year. I had visited a few friends in the hospital shortly after their deliveries. Other than looking sleepy and a tad bit parched, their bodies had not really appeared to have gone through hours of screaming and pushing – in short, massive trauma. They had hidden from me the world of episiotomies, incontinence, hemorrhoids, vagina-numbing sprays, and adult diapers. Instead they handed me their newborns and in between coos they would look at me and say, "When's your turn? Don't you want a little darling of your own?"

When I visited my sister, the room looked nothing short of a crime scene. She looked like she had been punched in the face several times and lay there almost lifeless. In between the gasps and fainting spells she looked over at me and said more than once, "Have 'em young."

I gave her a "you must be clinically insane" look and decided that it was not time to go off the pill just yet. If I had anything to say about it, I was going to try to preserve my private parts just a little longer.

In the meantime, there were still plenty of other reasons that made me ill at ease when thinking about having babies. First, there were the dreams. One dream I can still remember:

It was a normal, uneventful day and I had spent it like I would any other day – eating with friends, doing the laundry, running a few errands, and maybe some shopping. I come home only to find a newborn (my newborn apparently) screaming at the top of his lungs because his negligent mother had forgotten about him for the last 24 hours.

<End Scene>

I woke up in cold sweats. What if I had a baby and was a complete and utter failure as a mother? What if I was incapable of doing simple tasks like heating up a bottle correctly or changing a diaper? (A two-year-old once laughed in my face when she realized I had put her diaper on backwards and had forgotten her diaper cream. A toddler was giving me instructions.) Or worse yet, what if I was so exhausted from the lack of sleep that I happened to drop the baby? I am way too young to have Social Services after me or to go to prison. I would become someone's bitch for sure.

Next, there were the parents of newly born or young children. These were the couples that looked like they just had ten years of life sucked out of them. They would refer to their pre-baby days as "the good ol' days." They would have fights to astronomical proportions and at moments looked as though they could tear each other apart with their bare hands. They were clearly in survival mode.

And I was happily childless. I still enjoyed spending time with Kevin. We had the freedom to do whatever, eat whatever, spend whatever, and go wherever. A newly married friend of mine once said, "Why ruin a good thing?" and I thought surely she must have been speaking words from God. Kevin and I still liked each other, and I wanted to keep it that way.

And then there was the sinking feeling that having a baby would mean that life would be over as I knew it. That is, *my life* would be over – Kevin, of course, would still go on to lead his life. He would still be able to devote time to his career and go out with his boys; meanwhile, I would be at home with an inconsolable baby literally sucking the life out of me. Say goodbye to all of my dreams, hopes, and aspirations; hello to poopie diapers, engorged breasts, and sleep training.

To say I was afraid to become a mom would be the biggest understatement of the decade.

Even when we started "trying" (i.e., what married people say when they are having lots and lots of unprotected sex), I wasn't exactly shouting from the rooftops, "I am now ready to be a mom!" I was only a little less scared of the idea and had just enough courage to stop taking the pill and "wait and see" what would happen.

And *it* happened. And life as I knew it did change.

But it wasn't the change I had expected. Instead of terror and fear, I was elated. Each day I carefully thought about what I was doing and putting into my body so that our baby would be safe. I cut out all of my favorite things without complaint (e.g., sushi, coffee, deli meats). When I felt queasy and exhausted or when I was waking up in the middle of the night to go to the bathroom, I was excited to be showing pregnancy symptoms and hoped that meant our baby was strong. And sometimes I would sing the song Phoebe from *Friends* sang after implanting the tiny little embryo in her uterus:

Are you in there little fetus?
In nine months will you come greet us?
I will buy you some Adidas.

I began to have different kinds of dreams – dreams of what our baby would look like and what kind of parents Kevin and I would be. I had dreams of calling our baby by name, of cradling and smelling our baby. I thought about April, the month we would have met our baby, and how spring would be the perfect time for our baby to enter the world.

The funny thing is that I could not have imagined how this baby would rock my world and turn it upside-down in just the two short weeks I knew I was pregnant. I had no idea that I could be so captured with just the thought of our baby without even having been able to meet him or her. I was not aware that I could love so fast, so hard, and so deeply until now.

That's the funny thing.

THE OTHER SIDE

MARCH 7, 2011

Today marks the beginning of my 25th week of pregnancy. These last six months have been filled with a flurry of emotions – shock, fear, excitement, anxiety, and most of all – unspeakable joy.

Learning that I was pregnant so soon after a loss was more difficult than I would have expected. Early in the pregnancy, every week was filled with terror and questions: Is the baby alright? Am I eating enough? Should I be sleeping earlier? Nightly vomiting sessions actually provided me some sort of emotional relief, while sleeping through the night and not being jolted awake at 3 A.M. with an urge to pee would cause a near meltdown. Fear of losing another baby was at the forefront of my mind, and I was dangerously towing the line between "normal" and Crazy Town.

During these last six months I found it difficult to put into words how I was feeling about the pregnancy. Friends had encouraged me to write, and even Baby Center gave me weekly reminders to "write a pregnancy memory." I have been reluctant and afraid to be honest about how much in love I am with this baby whom I have never met, and how excited I am to meet her in a few short months.

Having been on the other side of pregnancy – miscarriage, grief, and loss – has made me much more grateful for the life that is now blooming inside of me. Her kicks and punches always bring a smile to my face, as she reminds me that she is growing, alive and well.

I am counting down the weeks until I get to meet our daughter. I am overwhelmed with love and excitement, and it is so hard to still hold loosely to this pregnancy, this baby. I imagine it will be even harder once she makes her entrance into this world. God help me.

THE WAITING GAME

MARCH 27, 2011

Pregnancy, at times, can feel like an interminable game of waiting.

Of course, there is the road to pregnancy that can seem endless, fraught with challenges and heartbreak. This is when "trying" does not result in what it is "supposed to" – a happy, joyous pregnancy – and each month is met with tears and disappointment.

With this pregnancy, each day and week of the first trimester slowly inched along. I was impatient when my doctor's office told me I needed to wait until the 8-week mark to meet with my doctor. And I anxiously awaited the 13-week mark – then I would be able to breathe a sigh of relief knowing that I was in the "safe(r) zone." Then there was the 20-week anatomy scan where we would find out if we were having a boy or a girl (during which our baby conveniently had her legs crossed). More scans, more tests. I am typically a good test-taker, but somehow I managed to fail the 3-hour glucose tolerance test and wound up with gestational diabetes.

The countdown now is 12 weeks and 5 days to go, or 89 days to be exact.

This waiting period reminds of the engagement period. You experience much of the same feelings – fear, excitement, anxiety, and anticipation for the BIG DAY (more like fear and dread of my private parts being ripped open). There are meltdowns (for which I would like to take a moment and thank progesterone – the pregnancy hormone that makes you certifiably insane), sometimes stress, and thoughts of – How on earth am I going to pay for all of this? What will she look like? Will my nipples bleed? What does no sleep *really* do to your psyche? Checklists, things to do, time-lines, registries, babymoons, and showers.

I can hardly believe that my third trimester is already here. I hope my baby doesn't look like an alien. My heart will burst for her anyway.

"Wishing and hoping and thinking and praying…"

CHANGE OF PLANS

APRIL 12, 2011

No matter how hard we try to organize or plan for things, some things remain absolutely out of our control.

April 12th was the date our first baby was scheduled to make his or her entrance into this world. What we weren't expecting was a change of plans.

Today I sit and anxiously wait to meet our daughter in a few short weeks. And I remember the baby I carried and lost last August.

> *"And now, isn't it wonderful all the ways in which this distress has goaded you closer to God? You're more alive, more concerned, more sensitive, more reverent, more human, more passionate, more responsible. Looked at from any angle, you've come out of this with purity of heart."*
> The Message – 2 Corinthians 7:11

TV LESSONS

APRIL 21, 2011

I have just recently discovered the goodness of Netflix. I am aware I'm a few years behind. I'm a little slow that way.

At the prompting of our friend, Kevin and I started watching *Friday Night Lights* on Netflix. Since Kevin's a basketball coach, it makes sense we would gravitate towards movies and television shows about sports and coaching.

Last night we watched an episode titled "I Think We Should Have Sex" in which Coach Taylor's daughter contemplates having sex with her quarterback boyfriend. She's only 15 years old.

I felt our little girl dancing around inside of my belly and wondered how we might broach *that* fun subject.

Everything I learned about sex came from peers, *Cosmopolitan* magazine, and *Beverly Hills 90210*. I remember watching with nail-biting anticipation when Donna Martin and David Silver finally decided to "do it."

So I asked Kevin, "How are we supposed to know how to parent a teen? We were never parented ourselves!"

And he said, "That's what TV is for."

Adolescent angst scares the bejeezus out of me, and my baby isn't even out of the womb yet.

Perhaps I should first worry about how I am supposed to squeeze a human being out of my private parts. Nine more weeks to go.

ARTS & CRAFTS

APRIL 22, 2011

I may just be the least crafty person I know. I am about as artistic as a three-year-old ... except I can color between the lines. I gave up on visual art in the 1st grade and learned early on it wasn't exactly my gifting.

When I look at other moms coming up with art projects and creating all sorts of goodies for their children – scrapbooks, costumes, outfits, blankets, party favors – I am in **awe**.

My sister tried to teach me how to knit once (maybe twice) and I failed miserably. I could barely pay attention long enough to understand what her hands were doing with the needle. I attempted one stitch before I dropped the ball of yarn and put my needles away for good.

I was once talking with a mom friend of mine about how I would never be able to give my child a homemade anything. She said, "When you have kids, of course you will!"

No, I won't.

That is like saying to someone who has never cooked anything besides rice and instant noodles that when she gets married, she will be able to cook delicious meals for her husband. You can ask Kevin how well that turned out. Did I also mention I just recently learned how to boil an egg?

But maybe I should not be too hard on myself. Perhaps I won't be able to hand-make all of her Halloween costumes or knit her blankets and dolls; no, I will pay the many talented people of this world to do that for me. But I can spend my time writing down memories and incredibly embarrassing stories about her and bind them in a book for her amusement later on when she is able to appreciate them. I can provide entertainment, and who can put a price on entertainment?

FERTILELAND

MAY 4, 2011

Fertileland is a topic that has been sitting on my "great ideas" notepad since last September. The original idea for this essay came from a place of mourning shortly after my miscarriage. A friend of mine, who is no stranger to grief and loss, gently warned me, "Everyone will be pregnant. Cousins, celebrities, best friends ... **your grandma might be pregnant**."

And it certainly appeared to be so.

In the days and weeks following the miscarriage, it seemed like every week I was hearing about someone newly pregnant. Every other Facebook post seemed to be an update of sonograms, pregnancy cravings, or "We're having a ___!" In fact, I found out on Facebook that another friend is pregnant just five seconds ago.

While such news is supposed to be joyous and celebratory, I was surprised at how excruciating it was for me to hear. I felt like everyone was throwing their vibrant, fertile wombs in my face, while I was left to cry in the corner, wondering why our baby was not one we would ever meet. Truth be told, I began to "hide" all of the pregnant ladies from my Facebook Newsfeed, and did a little bit of hiding on my own. I hated myself for my lack of enthusiasm and excitement and my insincere "Congratulations," and I figured this was the only way to keep sane while still grieving the loss of our little one.

Now being on the other side, hearing that someone is pregnant elicits a much different response. I can joyfully participate in the squeals, hugs, and congratulatory remarks, while hoping and praying that I get to meet their healthy little one.

And since I'm such a lists person, I created a list of all those who have been (and have delivered) or are currently pregnant during my pregnancy. The number is up to 32. I am thrilled that so many are blooming with life and have marriages flourishing in the bedroom.

NESTING

MAY 16, 2011

In the early days of pregnancy, one of the most frequently asked questions was, "So how are you feeling?"

These days, the questions people ask the most are "Are you ready?" and "Do you wish the baby was just here already?"

The short answer to both of these questions is a loud and emphatic "NO."

Let's not even talk about parenthood yet. I'm not sure anyone ever feels "ready" to become a parent – to be ready to love, nurture, protect, discipline, teach, and be responsible for another human being ... maybe only those who are incredibly naive and extremely self-assured (like all of the girls on the MTV show *16 and Pregnant*).

And I'm not the slightest bit ready to broach the subject of labor and delivery yet either, so please spare me your horror stories about how your anus ripped to your vagina after three hours of pushing (or your boastful stories about how you labored at home until you were seven centimeters dilated and when you got to the hospital your baby just popped right out). I figure, since I have little to no control over what transpires during my labor and delivery, I won't waste my wakeful hours worrying about it. Although, I did look Kevin straight in the face yesterday and asked him to pop me a Valium or shoot me with a tranquilizer gun when the time comes to leave for the hospital.

So what *have* I spent my time doing?

I believe it is commonly referred to as "nesting."

And if by nesting, you mean running around like a chicken with its head cut off, then yes, that is what I have been doing.

"They" say nesting begins around month 5, which I would say is pretty accurate. It started with my obsession with our floor. If I saw a hair on the floor, I would pick it up. If there were crumbs, I would wipe them up as well. Pretty soon you would see me making my rounds through the kitchen, hunched over with an antibacterial wipe, desperately trying to catch any dirt, grime, or stray hairs. Using a vacuum would be too easy.

Then it became my incessant need to make sure the house was tidy before going ANYWHERE. If this meant being 15 minutes late because I had to make sure all of the remote controls were facing the correct direction and the couch cushions were aligned properly, then so be it. I had more important things to do.

These days it means going through all of our baby items, mentally cataloging what we have, what we need, and what I can return while asking myself the following questions:

Will the baby really need all of these toys?

How many "newborn" onesies does a baby really need? What if she outgrows them in two weeks?

Do I like this crib sheet?

If I dress her in an all-green onesie, will people mistake her for a boy?

Will I need a manual pump *and* an electric pump?

<Insert unsolicited advice here.>

Tonight, I spent the last three hours moving boxes of diapers and wipes from upstairs to downstairs, shuffling various baby items around from room to room, unpacking the 0–3 month clothes and separating them into colors and whites (since I'll be going to buy Dreft tomorrow and Kevin promises to put the dresser together), and creating more mental checklists of things to do.

Paint – check. Carpet cleaning – check. Dresser – to be built tomorrow. Crib – next week. Install car seat. Make an appointment with the local police station to make sure car seat is installed correctly. Pack hospital bag.

I feel like a crazy person, and yet all of this is completely normal. At least, that's what I'm told. Or what "they" say.

ALMOST . . .

JUNE 9, 2011

I've got about two weeks and some change until my estimated due date.

Some "new" things I've been experiencing as of late:

Leg cramps. They sort of feel like your legs are being chopped off, usually occurring in the middle of the night or just as I am waking up in the morning.

Restlessness. I think we completed everything on my baby checklist by June 1. Paint – check. Carpet/upholstery cleaning – check. House cleaning – check. Car seat installation – check. Buy last-minute items/return/exchange items – check. Diapers/wipes – check. Crib/dresser – check. Check, check, check. What else? *Must keep moving.* Sometimes I'll go to Target or Babies"R"Us just to walk around and check for the hundredth time that I have everything I need.

Nesting bug. As mentioned before, this started around month 5 and has not waned since. If anything, I have become even more of a dictator about keeping the house spotless. I even spent an hour landscaping on our patio (behind Kevin's back) because *of course* the baby will **not** appreciate coming home to a house with weeds and overgrown shrubs.

Mixed emotions. Fear, excitement, anxiety ... The other morning I woke up thinking, "Oh GOD, I'm having contractions!" only to realize it was just last night's dinner.

COUNTDOWN

JUNE 20, 2011

I feel like a time bomb waiting to explode.

I suppose you could read that as a figure of speech, but I envision a baby exploding out of my private parts ... like something out of a science fiction movie.

At first I was scared I might go into labor at work since I was working up until one week before my due date. Now I'm wondering if I will have to wait until July to see my baby. Something in the middle would be nice.

These last few days have been filled with an endless amount of cleaning, home improvement projects, and movie-going. In the last two weeks I have watched *Bridesmaids*, *Midnight in Paris*, *X-Men: First Class*, *Kung Fu Panda 2*, and *Super 8*. Today we'll be watching *Fast Five*, tomorrow *Water for Elephants*, and *Bad Teacher* on Friday if the baby still hasn't made her appearance. *Tree of Life* is also on the menu, although I have no idea what it's about except that Brad Pitt is starring in the movie, which is reason enough to watch it.

Late last night, after my fourth load of laundry and as I was washing dishes for the third time that day, I noticed a tear in one of our dish-washing gloves. I asked Kevin what time Target opens so that I could go and buy a pair.

"You want to go to Target as soon as they open so you can buy dish-washing gloves?"

My husband thinks I'm crazy, but I think it makes perfect sense to stock the house with everything we might possibly need for the next three months.

All this to keep my mind distracted from constantly wondering when we will get to hold our daughter. I could easily think about that during my wakeful hours.

So now we wait.

A NEW BEGINNING: OUR BIRTH STORY

On Sunday, June 26th at 8:34 P.M. our daughter decided to make her debut. True to form, she arrived promptly on her due date, although we were getting antsy and impatient, thinking she might decide to be fashionably late.

5:40 A.M. – I am in the middle of dreaming I am in labor. Actually, it is more like a nightmare. Dream doctor tells me I do not have time to get an epidural and that I would have to feel the full extent of this human being squeezed out of my private parts.

5:44 A.M. – I wake up for no apparent reason. Maybe it is the nightmare. Or maybe it is God telling me it is go time.

5:45 A.M. – I feel something trickle out down there, and wonder if this could mean my water has broken. I rule out urine since it's been at least ten years since I've wet the bed.

5:50 A.M. – We call my OB and she says to start heading over to Labor & Delivery. I can hardly believe today is the day! We make sure everything is packed and head to the hospital.

6:15 A.M. – The nurses run something called a "fern test" to see if my water has truly broken. If it has, I can stay; if not, back to the house I go.

9:00 A.M. – They confirm my water bag has ruptured and start me on an IV and pitocin to regulate my contractions and get the labor going. (I am already contracting on my own, but the contractions are still irregular.) When I entered the hospital, I was 3 centimeters dilated, 50% effaced. The contractions definitely feel like menstrual cramps, but are still bearable.

1:00 P.M. – The anesthesiologist comes in and asks if I would like my epidural now since he is going in for a C-section and will not be available for at least another hour. Since I'm scared the pain will get worse, I agree to get it now.

*This was probably the scariest part of the whole labor process for me. I know thousands of women get the epidural, but I have always had this irrational fear that getting a shot in my spine might leave me paralyzed. Once the anesthesiologist was finished administering the epidural, I burst into tears and scared the crap out of him.

Soon after I receive my epidural, they realize I am not dilating because my water bag is not fully broken. Once they completely break my water bag, I begin dilating immediately.

6:00 P.M. – The nurse tells me I am at 10 centimeters but we are going to "labor down" for another hour to allow my contractions to bring the baby further down the birth canal (rather than have me push for an extra hour).

7:30 P.M. – The nurse tells me I am ready to begin pushing. My teeth start to chatter. Before we begin, she advises me to push like I have been constipated for the last ten months (which is not completely untrue). I push three pushes with each contraction, each push lasting ten seconds. I feel like my face is going to explode.

8:30 P.M. – They call in the OB and I know our baby is almost here! Once the doctor is in, everything happens so fast. With my last push I feel immediate relief and I see my baby's face for the first time at 8:34 P.M. "You made it!" They put her on my chest and I can hardly believe she is finally here.

Overwhelmed, exhausted, elated, amazed, and overall – **grateful**.

It's been a whirlwind.

CATCHING MY BREATH

SEPTEMBER 2011

I am glad I managed to write SOMETHING down about my birth story in those first couple of weeks after birth. I am fairly certain I would not have remembered everything in detail if I had waited to write about it, what with "mommy brain" and all – which, I have discovered, is a REAL thing. I can barely recall what I ate for dinner last night. I think it was Anne Lamott who said when you give birth to a baby, 15% of your brain comes out with it. Whole words fall out of your head, you forget how to get from point A to point B, and you long for the days when uninterrupted sleep was not a distant memory and you were able to function as a normal human being. Did you know interrogators use sleep deprivation as a torture tool for prisoners of war? Welcome to motherhood.

I actually started this essay about a week ago and it has been sitting in my "drafts" folder. I have also been taking notes in my "great ideas" folder about things I wanted to remember or write about the first few weeks of motherhood. I am still debating whether or not to write about them for fear of 1) scaring the daylights out of those who are pregnant or ever wish to have children and 2) making a rash decision to get my tubes tied and close up shop forever. If you want the details, let me know. Or perhaps I will be brave (or mean) enough to write about them in due time.

Now that I am beginning to enjoy my girl more and feel less like I am losing my mind, I think I can begin to write again.

BABY STEPS

OCTOBER 2011

I was originally going to title this essay "re-education" until I remembered the term is often used as a euphemism for brainwashing.

ReLEARNING ...

Having a baby forces you to learn a host of new things. First of all, you have to learn how to FEED your baby, which is no simple task! And once your nipples have stopped bleeding and have turned to leather, you need to learn how to SLEEP your baby. And then there are the twenty or so diapers a day you will need to become a master at changing – quickly enough to avoid being hit with a stream of urine or poop. Being a first-time mother requires on-the-job training in a bleary-eyed world where you are lucky if you can get two consecutive hours of sleep at a time in those first weeks. And don't waste your time reading any parenting books, because I guarantee you will not remember any of it once your baby is born. In fact, I recommend tossing all of those books out the window, or at least storing them away until you are getting at least enough sleep to be able to synthesize material. I must have read the same chapter in a sleep training book at least twenty times in those first six weeks, and I thought I was reading a foreign language.

I did not realize I would need to re-learn so many things once I had a baby.

I did not know I would need to train myself to sleep without jumping out of bed and waking up to every tiny sound just to make sure my baby was still alive and breathing. Or learn when and how much I needed to eat so I would not wake up starving at 3 A.M., because breastfeeding will do that to you! Or learn how to steam treat my ass without burning it (i.e., a sitz bath). Or learn how to **GET OUT OF THE HOUSE**, which is probably one of those things you will want to learn quickly so you do not officially lose your mind. I was close.

Malcolm Gladwell says it takes 10,000 hours to master a skill. So according to Gladwell, I am about 25% of the way there. Maybe by baby's first birthday, I will begin to feel like I can do this mom thing ... or something that resembles doing this mom thing.

These days I am beginning to feel like the fog is lifting, and though there are still some sleepless nights I am able to enjoy my Miss Sassafras more each day.

Love is wonderful thing / Make ya smile through the pouring rain.
– Michael Bolton

WHAT A FEELING

OCTOBER 25, 2011

Tomorrow marks four months since my baby was born.

There were days when I thought I would never make it to tomorrow. I was surprised to find we were both alive and well at the four-week mark. I was sure that at any moment I might keel over and never wake up. I was so sleep-deprived I would scratch at my eyes just to make sure my senses were still intact.

The best way I can describe those first couple months of motherhood is that it was a complete **shock** – a shock to the body, a shock to my identity, and ultimately a shock to my life. I felt more like a slave than a mother. I thought living in a three-hour world would drive me mad for sure. My life became a series of feeding, burping, holding, rocking, and diaper-changing sessions, and somewhere in between I was supposed to find time to eat and sleep. When I looked in the mirror I wondered, "Who is that crazy homeless lady staring back at me?" Predictability and schedules were thrown out the window. I felt like I had lost control – lost my mind – and my life was over.

This was not quite the picture of motherhood I had imagined before Aliya entered my life and rocked my world to the very core.

While I knew intellectually that motherhood would be an adjustment – and a difficult one at that – perhaps in some corner of my mind I thought motherhood would be a perpetual state of bliss because I wanted a baby so badly. Instead, what I found was motherhood was more like a day that never ends, where I wanted someone to punch me in the face just so I could feel something. It was not long before I felt guilty, worthless, and like a complete and utter failure. If all of the girls on *Teen Mom* could do it, why couldn't I?

Moms repeatedly told me – **"It WILL get better."** I thought they were all psycho sadistic liars who were cruel enough to not warn me how miserable this all was. Or they were all extremely well-adjusted with babies who never cried and always slept.

But slowly, things did get better.

She got bigger. She started to smile. And miracle of miracles – she learned how to **SLEEP**. And so did I.

These days I can hardly get enough of her.

What a feeling in my soul
Love burns brighter than sunshine
Brighter than sunshine
Let the rain fall, I don't care
I'm yours and suddenly you're mine
Suddenly you're mine
And it's brighter than sunshine
– Aqualung, "Brighter than Sunshine"

SLEEP

NOVEMBER 2011

It's 4 P.M. and I'm still in my pajamas.

Since Miss Sass has been going through her 4-month sleep regression, I thought I would dedicate today's essay to *sleep*.

You know how they say absence makes the heart grow fonder? Or how you never really know how much you love something (or someone) until it's gone? I'm sure "they" probably weren't talking about sleep, but "they" probably weren't sleep-deprived first-time parents either.

I never realized how much I loved sleep until it was gone.

I should have listened to those nurses who told me to sleep during labor. "You'll need all your energy for pushing!" What they failed to mention was that I would not be sleeping for the next two months.

At the hospital I probably slept a total of five hours during our two-night stay. And as we headed home, I thought, "Oh, it'll be nice to finally get some sleep in my bed now without those nurses coming in every hour!"

Foolish.

During those first two weeks with the baby at home I was running off of pure adrenaline. I was so thrilled to be with my daughter and have her home. In fact, during one of my first middle-of-the-night feedings I wept as I stared at my beautiful baby girl. I was so grateful, and having experienced a miscarriage with the first pregnancy I knew being able to carry and deliver a healthy baby was nothing short of a miracle. Two weeks later, I was crying for other reasons.

Even when by some miracle my Miss Sass was sleeping, I could not sleep. Perhaps it had to do with my funky brain chemistry or hormone levels after childbirth, but my anxiety levels were off the charts. If she slept for two hours during the day I would think, "Wake her up, she's not going to sleep tonight!" Or if she slept for 30 minutes I would think, "Good God, why is she not sleeping?" If she cried while I was nursing, I would wonder, "Is she still hungry? Did she eat too much? Is the milk coming out too fast for her? Or maybe it's not fast enough?" If she pooped a lot it was, "Does she have diarrhea? Does her tummy hurt?" If she pooped too little it was, "Is she dehydrated? Do I need to feed her more? Maybe she's constipated?"

What didn't help was when well-meaning doctors or moms would tell me to just sleep when the baby sleeps. Or, "Gee, you really need to rest." You think? Oh, just sleep when the baby sleeps, that's all! Thanks for the tip!

When you are not sleeping, each day feels like an eternity and you begin to wonder if you're going to be able to live another day with a little life-sucker attached to your chest. And you look at every mom you know with wonder and amazement and ask, "How on earth did you survive this?"

Because moms are amazing, that's how.

HEIGH-HO, HEIGH-HO

DECEMBER 2, 2011

Today is my last official day of maternity leave.

There have been so many different emotions swirling around this past week – sadness, anxiety, excitement, fear, guilt, and anticipation just to name a few.

Moms forewarned me I wouldn't really know how I would feel about returning to work until Aliya was here. They were right.

I've flip-flopped a few times already since she's been born. Days after she was born, I couldn't imagine ever leaving her. And then about three weeks later, I was sure I was ready to go back to work, where I might find a bit of my "old" self, lingering around somewhere. Five months later, I am **somewhere in between**.

I just love my Sassafras to pieces.

THE LITTLE THINGS

JANUARY 2, 2011

Growing a baby has given me a newfound appreciation for the little things – beginning in pregnancy and into the first year of Miss Sassafras's life.

During pregnancy, I loved reading about all the ways our baby was developing in my belly. First, she learned how to curl her fingers and toes. And then before I knew it, she was giving me full-fledged punches and kicks each day to remind me that she was growing strong and there to keep me company (**for the rest of my life**).

And then she was born. And I have been able to see her grow, change, and develop right before my very eyes.

First she learned how to track with her eyes. "Do you see me? Do you see Mommy?"

Then she learned how to hold her head up for more than ten seconds at a time.

Then she learned how to **smile**. And then I died.

Then she learned how to sleep on her own without Mommy or Daddy shuffling up and down the hallway in a sleep-deprived stupor. This was nothing short of a miracle.

Soon after she learned how to roll from her back onto her tummy. And then we became sleep-deprived again.

Then she learned how to grab and take hold of things. In the past few months she has become an expert grabber (my hair is her object of choice), roller, laugh machine, and solid-food eater. In recent weeks she has learned to vigorously shake her head "no" ("doree doree" for you Koreans), and I am getting the sense that it will be a matter of weeks before she begins to crawl. For now, she is a swivel machine, which means that one minute she will be pointing north, and then 15 seconds later she will be pointing southwest.

I am awaiting many more "firsts" with my girl – her first words, first steps ... and I know the day will come when she can wipe her own ass. That will be revolutionary.

MOMMY-ISMS

Here are a few things I have learned or noticed since becoming a mommy:

The amount of spit-up in my hair or on my clothing will determine if it is wash-worthy.

The amount of spit-up in her hair or on her clothing will determine if it is wash-worthy.

I will eat something that has fallen on the floor if it means getting out the door faster.

My reaction to being peed on: "Pee is sterile."

I can do all the animal sounds during one feeding of solids. Twice. And a song. Or two.

I stopped saying, "My child/baby will never ..."

When people without children say, "I understand ..." I laugh in their face. Or in my head.

I appreciate SILENCE.

I have become a neat FREAK.

My new hangout curfew is 7:30 P.M.

I have learned that poops-up-the-back most often happen right before work or in a public place.

Boogers, sharts, pooplosions, and projectile vomit no longer faze me.

I have learned to do things one-handed.

I think anyone who is pregnant or has baby urges before her child turns one is batshit crazy. Or super. But probably crazy.

***The other day I met a woman with a 10-month old who is pregnant with her second child, due in two weeks. *<insert expletive>* She and her husband must have had "relations" just seconds after she gave birth to the first one.

I cherish sleep. I will never complain about only getting five hours of sleep again.

7 MONTHS

JANUARY 27, 2012

At 7 months, my sweet Sassafras just passed the half-year mark and is growing at light speed.

Every week she is learning something new. A few weeks ago, she started doing this thing where she scrunches her entire face when something delights her.

And just this past week, she began using her pincer grasp and successfully put a Super Puff IN HER MOUTH. She is also learning how to hold her own bottle, although most of the time she forgets to hold it up and instead pushes it down, causing the nipple to fly out and spray her entire face (and mine) with milk. We are working on it.

For the past couple of weeks, she has also been desperately trying to master crawling. I think it may be a matter of days before we have a crawler on our hands, but for now she will continue to develop buff arms from doing push-ups all day long.

At this point in time, she still has zero teeth, but I swear one morning she is going to wake up and have a full set of teeth. That will scare the crap out of me.

In the last month, we have enjoyed seeing Aliya's personality develop. There is no doubt she is her father's daughter. She feels things intensely and she is not afraid to let you know! She loves being with others, is extremely curious and observant, and is a determined little girl. She likes to win people over with her gummy smile and her head tilt. She already loves to babble and if you are wondering where her volume comes from, I have one guess.

I am learning to slow down and enjoy moments with my daughter because I am realizing that they are fleeting. The first couple months of motherhood were marked heavily by postpartum depression – an unexpected, terrifying, and dark time in my life, which I hope to never revisit. Most days I was trying to survive, to stay afloat just long enough to keep from drowning and losing myself (and my sanity) altogether. My heart still aches when I think about it, but I am so thankful for my sweet Sassafras. Nothing could have prepared me for this, but every day my heart is expanding and I am changing because of my little girl.

QUESTIONS YOU SHOULD NOT ASK

This essay was inspired by a recent conversation with a dear friend of mine about lame ass questions (sometimes well-meaning or otherwise clueless) people ask all too often. And since she is too nice to say these things to the general public, I volunteered to share this information as a public service announcement.

> *Are you pregnant? Are you pregnant **yet**? Isn't it about time you guys had kids? TICK TOCK!*

If you have to ask (multiple times), chances are that you probably are not close with the person you're asking. Some women, particularly with their first pregnancy, like to keep things under wraps during the first trimester while the chances of miscarriage are much higher. If she is pregnant, she will probably tell you when she is good and ready to share the news! And if she is not pregnant, it may be worthwhile to consider reasons WHY. Perhaps she does not WANT to be pregnant! And if she does want to be pregnant and is not pregnant, she may be desperately TRYING to get pregnant and struggling privately with the frustrations/heartbreak every single month she learns that she is still NOT pregnant. So thanks for the reminder, but still **not** pregnant! Nope! Not this month. Not yet! Maybe never?

***A better question might be, "So are you thinking about having kids?"

> *(MEN asking): So how is breastfeeding going?*

First of all, the asker of this question assumes I am actually breastfeeding. Any mom will know what a big fat can of worms this is – breastfeeding vs. formula feeding, "breast is best", La Leche League (a.k.a. the BOOB Nazis), pumping, bottle-feeding, nipple confusion, etc. And second of all – **REALLY**? You want to talk about my BOOBS right now? Should I tell you about how engorged they are and how they feel like a pile of rocks? Or how my nipples have turned to leather after being sucked on by a newborn for eight hours a day? Or how I become a standing milkshake after a warm shower? Or about all the times I sprayed poor baby's face because that milk just SHOT right out of me! HAHAHA, that was HILARIOUS!

We never talked about my boobs before, so why now? It's creepy and gross.

I don't ask you about your penis, so don't ask me about my boobs.

What is even more awesome is when a dude says, "Yeah, breastfeeding can be really hard." Oh yeah? Why don't you tell me all about it?

So is motherhood everything you dreamed of and more? Are you enjoying every single millisecond of your new bundle of joy?

OH MY GOD. YES. I cannot tell you how much I enjoy *not* sleeping. Have you ever not slept for days? Scratch that. WEEKS? It is a fantastic mixture of delirium and insanity, on top of the new responsibility of taking care of a tiny little human being who just burst out of your private parts and is 100% dependent on YOU. Not to mention the projectile vomiting, tar poop, diarrhea, pooplosions, poop poop poop, pee pee pee, and crying that I have now become accustomed to all day, every day.

I love my baby. I really do.

To their credit, those asking this particular question do not have kids.

***A better question might be, "So how is motherhood?"

8 MONTHS

FEBRUARY 28, 2012

In Sassafras's first months as a newborn, I could not wait for her to get to this stage, and now that she is here I would like for the time to go by just a bit more slowly. **THIS stage, I will miss.** I am fairly certain I will never enjoy/miss the newborn stage. I will not be joining the ranks of mamas with 4+ children (unless God has other plans, like a virgin birth or something). I am not super-human like you.

It seems Sassafras has begun to master the skills she was just starting to venture into in the previous month. She is crawling around everywhere and is now trying to climb and pull herself up. She thinks she can do this with her arms and her face, but has yet to realize that her legs exist to help her stand. I hope she doesn't realize this for a few more months.

She can hold her own bottle! Now when she sees her bottle, she does her bottle dance, which essentially involves hyperventilating, bouncing up and down, and foot kicks. And then she stretches her arms out and opens her mouth wide to make sure that bottle lands exactly where it's supposed to land.

During her bedtime bottle, we have also started doing this thing where we raise our eyebrows at each other, scrunch our faces, and then laugh. It makes me feel like we have inside-jokes. She thinks I am the funniest mommy in the world, and I think she is the funniest baby. The feeling is mutual.

Other new developments include waving, scrunching her face on cue, clapping, and signing "more." This is a most excellent development, as I prefer signing to blood curdling screams.

Separation anxiety has also been in full force for the last few months. It is both a blessing and a curse. When I was sharing with my sister that Aliya is going through separation anxiety and only wants Mommy she said, "Yes, but isn't it the *sweetest*?!" As exhausting as this is, I must admit it is a good feeling to know she knows me and thinks I rock.

As for her teeth, we are (all) still waiting for them to surface. For now, there is just a ton of drool and snot and we are still enjoying her gummy grin.

FATHERS AND DAUGHTERS

Last night we were talking about babies, children, teenagers, and how god-awful those adolescent years can be. A friend of ours was over at the house and he jokingly forewarned us about the teenage years. A colleague, earlier that day, gave me the exact same warning. She encouraged me to "enjoy it now before you become the enemy." Then she rolled her eyes. She has four kids.

Good God.

I am still young enough to remember my own teenage angst, although as I approach 30, it is becoming more of a distant memory. My dad wasn't exactly the over-protective, hands-on type, but one thing I will never forget is how he scared the daylights out of the boy I was dating at the time.

He did the right thing.

Kevin says he is going to buy a handgun solely for the purpose of cleaning it when Sassafras brings boys to the house. Our friend also suggested keeping a dagger around, or a butcher knife. Any other suggestions?

THINGS TO AVOID SAYING TO A FIRST-TIME MOM

1. "I'm SO tired!"

Unless you too have a newborn attached to your body 24 hours a day (or have experienced some similar form of sleep deprivation), chances are you are not that tired. You may think you are experiencing some semblance of tiredness, but until your body has gone through massive trauma, you are given (overnight) the responsibility of feeding and caring for another, and are (at best) sleeping in two-hour increments (or not at all if you are experiencing the wonderful insomnia and postpartum depression/anxiety that I experienced) for weeks on end, you are not *that* tired.

A friend of mine noted, even if someone were cruel enough to wake you up every two to three hours every night for two months, it would still not be anything close to what a new mom experiences in those first couple of months.

I cannot even conjure up the words to describe how horrific and miserable postpartum insomnia and sleep deprivation really is. *Pure torture* and *hell* are the only words that come to mind at the moment.

2. "You look tired!"

Yeah? No shit, Sherlock.

3. (To a new formula-feeding mom): "Awww ... don't worry. Your baby will survive."

Really? Because I thought I was feeding her poison.

4. "So what are you up to today?"

Feed, burp, change, rock, sleep, repeat.

5. "My baby still won't sleep through the night/sleep in his crib/sleep without being held/etc. and he is almost a year old!"

No, no ... please do not say such things. It makes me want to curl up in the fetal position and shout expletives.

6. *<Pointing to stomach>* **"Is there still a baby in there?"**

Only a man would have the gall to say this. That man would be my dad.

7. (People without children): **"I understand."**

No you don't. Shut up. Get out.

8. "So when will you be having #2?"

Perhaps when I have long forgotten the postpartum period with #1. i.e., Not any time in the near future.

9. "Just follow your maternal instinct!"

What maternal instinct? Where can I get one of those?

I'm sure there are others out there who actually have this. Unfortunately, I was not born with one. I have to learn by doing, and in those first few months, nothing was instinctual. I constantly questioned myself as many first-time moms do, wondering whether or not I was doing things "right" (whatever that means) or if my poor feeding/napping/rocking/changing skills were setting up my sweet daughter for a lifetime of instability/insecurity/health problems/destruction.

My therapist once told me, "You're not being graded for this." Perfectionist, Type A moms, I feel you. We suffer.

TO MY KNOCKED-UP FRIENDS

I cannot express how thrilled I am for you to be entering this journey of motherhood!

It is like you are joining a sorority of sisters who have all lived through ten months of bodily changes plus an additional six to twelve weeks (or more) of sleep deprivation, engorged breasts, and episiotomies.

And if we all lived through it to tell our stories, you will too. Don't you worry.

Somewhere along the way, you will find your maternal instinct. You will know your baby, and your baby will know you. And if it doesn't happen immediately, be kind to yourself. It takes time to build a relationship. And one day your baby will lock eyes with you and smile, and at that moment you realize that you would jump in front of a moving train to save this perfect, tiny little creature. And your heart expands to levels you were not even aware existed.

My friend Kate once told me, "Children teach us that we are not in control and that we have to depend on God day by day." It is the truth. I would imagine this lesson becomes harder to learn as your children approach adolescence and start becoming independent and making their own decisions – good and bad. But it is also true at 3 A.M. when your newborn shits all over herself for the third time in a row, just after you have given her a fresh diaper. Or when your baby suddenly gets a bout of hiccups lasting for fifteen minutes, just seconds before falling asleep. Those are the moments you throw your hands up to the sky and ask, "Why God, WHY?"

The sleepless nights will feel like an eternity, but **you will sleep again**. Time will resume its normal course and you will see how much faster it flies by with an infant. One day they learn to lift their heads. Then they smile. And then they can roll over. Soon they start sitting on their own, crawling away from you, and during those wardrobe and diaper changes that turn into a wrestling match you'll sit back and think, "Remember when you were just a little blob that couldn't move? Yeah." I have heard from other moms that with each stage/milestone, one thing gets easier and another thing gets harder. I just can't wait for toddlerdom.

All to say, I am *genuinely* excited and happy for you! To all of the mamas who had babies between July and December of 2011, I must confess, I feared for your lives. Instead of excitement, I felt terror and dread for you. I thought, "Watch out! Your newborn is going to END you!" I probably should not have been allowed to attend any baby showers during those months, because when asked at my friend's shower what the "most enjoyable thing about the first month of motherhood" was I answered, "Nothing. Nothing is enjoyable the first month."

Now I am three months shy of my baby's first birthday and I *cannot* imagine my life without her. Becoming a mother has been incredibly humbling, life-changing, and challenging, but I would not change *a single thing*.

It helps that she is cute. Hopefully you are all just as fortunate.

9 MONTHS

MARCH 27, 2012

Smiley Smilerson (a.k.a. Sassafras) just turned 9 months yesterday.

When she reached 8 months, she had just learned how to pull herself up. The first time she did it, I think we were all shocked. The look on her face went from excitement to terror within a matter of seconds once she realized she did not know how to get back down without free-falling backwards. It is pretty entertaining to watch her go from standing to sitting; she'll stick out her arm for balance, and it takes her about 15 seconds to *very* slowly lower her bottom and then plop down. Now when we greet her in the mornings, she is already standing and waiting for us.

Now we have a **cruising** baby, which means I am constantly having visions of her smacking her head on *everything*. She'll grab whatever she can get her hands onto to try to pull herself up and climb or walk, but the couch is usually her prop of choice as she side shuffles her way from one side of the living room to the other.

Sign language: By month 8 she was signing "more" and in the last week or two she has learned to sign for "milk." I have been trying to teach her the signs for "eat" and "please" but she isn't having any of it yet.

Teeth: She finally sprouted two tiny little teeth! I feel like she has been "teething" her entire life (since it was the only explanation I could think of for those "off" nights when we all didn't sleep), but since they have finally cut through she's been a champ. An extra drooly champ.

I have also been trying to read more to her these days. She is just starting to laugh and smile at the pictures, so I think she is getting the hang of it. I hope to incorporate this as a part of her daily routine.

The months just keep flying by and I can hardly keep up. Every month she is learning or doing something new. It is all too fast.

BABY PLAY DATES

A friend of mine once told me play dates are just as important for moms as they are for the children ... probably more so when they are infants and "playing" generally consists of staring at each other and blowing spit bubbles.

In the early months when I was still on maternity leave, play dates were a way for me to stay sane and bring some normalcy (and adult interaction) back into my life. They were not only a way for me to see what other babies were up to – what milestones they were hitting, what they were eating, how they were SLEEPING, etc. – but they also served as a mechanism for me to connect with other moms and vent frustrations, share fears and insecurities, and encourage one another. I never understood just how lonely motherhood could be and I did not realize how overwhelmed I would feel. From spending time with other moms and babies I quickly learned I was not alone in this; I was just a normal first-time mom (post postpartum depression) experiencing normal first-time mom feelings with a normal, healthy, and active baby.

Suffice it to say, I always look forward to play dates!

MY FIRST MOTHER'S DAY

MAY 17, 2012

For a man who hates commercialized holidays, KK went all out for my first (baby out of belly) Mother's Day!

I know we celebrated Mother's Day last year, but I cannot remember what we did. I remember there was coffee ...

Most memories pre-baby escape me. I blame this on months of sleep deprivation.

KK had planned on letting me sleep in, but he had stayed up until 3 A.M. making my card and preparing goodies for my Mother's Day brunch! So when I brought Aliya downstairs for her morning bottle/breakfast, I was surprised to see a bouquet of flowers on the table, as well as a fridge STUFFED with food. My stomach was growling with excitement. If you have ever experienced his food, you'll know why.

We went to church for the 9 A.M. service and I thought I would give the nursery a second try. The first time we put Sassafras in childcare, not even twenty minutes had gone by before our nursery number began flashing on the screen (i.e., SAVE US FROM YOUR CHILD). This past Sunday, she did GREAT! And absolutely no crying! My guess is she succumbed to the endless amount of Cheerios.

As soon as we got home, Chef KK hit the ground running and began preparing a delicious brunch – a bacon and spinach frittata, salad, toast, homemade cornbread muffins (served with strawberries he had glazed overnight with hand-whipped cream) – topped off with cocktails. For dinner, he trekked out to Whole Foods and made lobster and avocado salad, DELICIOUS crab cakes, and his famous jambalaya.

I went running that night to wash away the guilt of gluttony. It only half-worked.

In short, my very first Mother's Day was amazing.

I am beyond blessed. Okay, and maybe a little spoiled.

My mind is now racing with ideas for Father's Day. I am a competitive over-achiever by nature and KK has set the bar very high. Unfortunately, I do not have a crafty bone in my body, so even the thought of making a card from scratch is a bit nerve-wracking (although, I could enlist my almost 11-month-old to "help" and then it would be sweet and endearing vs. comical and sad). I will also need to consider expanding my cooking repertoire beyond the three things I am comfortable cooking if I plan on making him a nice meal.

11 MONTHS

MAY 29, 2012

Sleep: Teething has reared its ugly head, and we all lost a few nights of sleep last week. She is still on the same sleep schedule, but for a week straight the poor girl was having multiple night wakings from the pain/discomfort. The remedy: infant Tylenol + extra TLC from mama.

Sign language: Soon after learning "milk" and "more" she learned "please" (now everything is "more please"), and most recently she has been using "up" and "all done" when she is finished eating and wants out of her high chair. She also does "wash hands" and "sleep" and "no no." When she is deliriously tired, usually before bed time, she will say something like, "More please up milk all done wash hands sleepy time."

I suppose this is the baby equivalent to slurred speech.

Food: We are slowly adding more food to her repertoire with eggs (mainly egg yolks) being the most newly added item. She loves to eat, but lately towards the end of her meals she has begun to spit and blow raspberries, spraying whatever goodies she has in her mouth onto her unfortunate caregiver (usually me). I have to think that somehow the sensation feels good on her sore gums and she is not solely doing it to see how long it takes Mommy to burst into flames. She has also been practicing her pterodactyl imitation, which has made eating out more trying. We have gotten better at tuning her out, but I know we have overstayed our welcome once the dirty looks begin. Parenting rocks.

Personality: These days she takes a bit to warm up to new people as her separation/stranger anxiety heightens (as I am told it does around age one), but once she does, you are her friend for life. She is extremely playful and loves to make people smile. This past month, she began to vocalize when something upset her or she wanted something, which is new. Before you could distract her or take things away without her noticing too much, but now she wants what she wants and she is not afraid to let you know it.

Enter toddlerdom? I am afraid.

I believe God creates this very fun, cute stage from about six to eighteen months to help mothers forget the trauma of the first couple months and to prepare for the terrible twos and threes (and f#$!ing fours). It seems this period, while your baby is cute and cuddly (and not yet insane), would be a great time to procreate if you want to have more than one child – unless you are like me and actually like to sleep. Then, you might hold off for a while.

I cannot believe my baby will be turning ONE in less than a month. I never thought I would be so emotional about Aliya turning one, but I have been catching myself getting teary during my quiet moments with her, wondering where the time has gone and reflecting on how much she and I have both grown in the last year.

And after we throw Sassafras's one-year birthday party, KK and I will have a "we survived the first year" celebration of our own. Perhaps alcohol will be involved.

1 YEAR

JUNE 2012

Sassafras is now one year old! And we all lived to see this day!

I remember in the early months, in my depressed and anxiety-ridden state, I would count down each hour, day, and week. When she was four weeks old, I would stare at my baby and think, "Okay, we're both still alive. That's a good thing." At the time, I could not even imagine making it to year one (or month two for that matter). And yet, here we are.

I remember many moms telling me to "enjoy every moment." And it would make me cringe. I do not know a single person who enjoys sleep deprivation. And if you do, perhaps you have supernatural, other-worldly powers that us lay folks lack.

But I am beginning to understand how bittersweet it is to watch your child grow. And the sheer amount of learning and development that happens in that first year is amazing. I have many proud-mama moments, and I have caught myself saying, "Do you remember when she used to ..." reminding myself of how far my baby has come. I surprised myself with how emotional I became over Sassafras turning one. I was sad the time had gone by so quickly, and I wanted to hold onto my baby just a bit longer because I am sure each subsequent year will go by faster and faster. And then someone reminded me, "But there is so much to look forward to!" And then I was okay.

Of course, one day it will be great to have a child who can wipe her own ass and can speak in coherent sentences.

KK and I have begun a tradition of writing letters to Aliya on her birthday in hopes that one day she will have a collection of letters to look back on and see a glimpse of how much she was loved. This might be one of my favorite traditions.

The birthday party was a success, despite Sassafras's head cold that weekend. At least everyone else had a good time. I am fortunate to be surrounded by talented, creative, and helpful family and friends who essentially did everything (decorations, favors, set-up, tear-down, photography, etc.). I suppose I did 100% of the physical labor of pushing Aliya out into this world, so I was okay with it. I hate planning parties. I am the worst person to ask to throw any kind of bridal/baby/birthday party/shower/event. I am saying this as a public service announcement, and not to be self-deprecating.

A LETTER TO MY ONE-YEAR-OLD DAUGHTER

JUNE 26, 2012

To my dearest Aliya,

You are officially one year old! Happy birthday, daughter! It's hard to imagine that just one year ago, early in the morning, you were still in my belly and we were making our way over to the hospital, brimming with excitement to finally meet you. We had no idea what we were in for.

As a first-time mom I stumbled along for a bit before I finally found my way. For some unknown reason I was under the assumption that babies did what they were supposed to – eat, sleep, repeat. And when that didn't happen, I came to the shocking realization that you were your own little person with your own mind and you would do your own thing. You couldn't care less about whether or not you had just pooped – no, you would do it again just seconds after getting a fresh diaper. When I learned that I couldn't control you, I had a temporary moment(s) of insanity, but once we all learned how to sleep, life began to resume its normal course. But better. Because you were now a part of it.

I know people may think I am biased, but I am certain I am not. You, child, are one gorgeous baby. You are beautiful and so smart and expressive. You are empathetic, playful, and a joy to be around. You are funny. And fun. You are so many more things than your typical one-year-old could ever be. You amaze me every day. Your daddy and I cannot get enough of you. Sometimes when I am at work I stare at my pictures of you and they help me to momentarily forget all of the nonsense and shenanigans that exist there.

In this past year, you (and we) have grown so much! I can tell that you are desperately wanting and trying to communicate in adult conversations, but so far the only word you say is "play." And your most frequent signs are "more" and "please." One day you will learn that there is such a thing as too much of a good thing.

My favorite rituals are bath time and bed time. You love to splash around and pat your little belly in the water. And we have our little bedtime games. Sometimes we make eyes at each other. Or you'll put your little forehead against mine and we'll shake our heads. Or you'll put your head in the crook of my neck and I'll shake my head and you'll shake yours back and we laugh. We have our little games that are ours and I love it.

You have changed my world and have changed me for the better. My heart bursts for you, daughter. I hope you know how much your dad and I love you. This has been the best year of our lives, and we have so much more to look forward to. I love you, Aliya. Happy 1st birthday.

Love,
Mommy

14 MONTHS

AUGUST 27, 2012

Sassafras continues to grow at light speed, and I am just trying to soak in each fleeting moment with her. My favorite time of day is bed time, when it's just me and my girl. We have our collection of inside jokes, which I hope continues to grow over the years.

Language: She still uses signs for milk, more, up, and please, but is trying to say more words. Is it any surprise that my daughter's very first word was **PLAY**? She has a number of "words" that all of her caregivers understand but probably are not understandable to the general population.

For example, she says "boo" which most often means BOOK, but could also mean Pooh Bear, blueberries, spoon, or balloon depending on where she is pointing. Other words – mama (for food and for me), pa (for Daddy), hi, bubba (for bubble), wawa (for water), caca (for crackers/Cheerios), and a number of animal sounds. She also says "bow bay" which means "Brown Bear," her favorite book of all time. Everyone in our house now has this book memorized, including Sassafras. Thank you, Eric Carle.

I am constantly amazed by how much she understands. She is beginning to understand when we tell her "no" and she finally understands the concept of "yes." She nods her head with vigor, opens her eyes wide, and raises her eyebrows when she means "YES." She also does this when eavesdropping on conversations, as if she's listening intently or in agreement.

She absolutely loves when we sing to her, particularly songs with hand motions such as Twinkle Twinkle Little Star, Wheels on the Bus, and Itsy Bitsy Spider.

While she is a mirror image of her dad, I attribute her love of books and music to me. And her wild hair.

Walking: She was "cruising" for months on end, and I was in no hurry for her to start walking. She finally took her first steps around the 13-month mark and now takes delight in walking everywhere. Watch out.

Play: These days, Sassafras finds endless pleasure in taking things out, putting things in, and stacking items. It is impressive how quickly a toddler can destroy your living room, bedroom, kitchen, play room, etc. Imagine the Tasmanian Devil from Looney Tunes. She is a riot.

IT WAS THE BEST OF TIMES, IT WAS THE WORST OF TIMES

OCTOBER 4, 2012

During the first couple months of Sassafras's life, I was obsessed with sleep. Obsessed as in I thought about it in every waking moment, which on some days was anywhere from 20–22 hours a day.

The first two weeks were not terrible. I spent two nights in the hospital after a routine vaginal delivery where I probably slept a total of 5–6 hours for the entire stay. But I didn't care. I was ecstatic to be with my daughter after months of waiting. Then we got home and Sassafras slept and ate and slept and ate and pooped like most newborns do, pretty much on cue, every 2–3 hours. And she didn't slow down. And I was confronted with a fatigue and mental/physical exhaustion I had never known before. And in the logical part of my brain I knew mothers for centuries had survived this period and continued to procreate in spite of this, but in the irrational corner of my brain, damaged by sleep deprivation and insomnia, I believed I would not survive. The early days were forever long, and if you have ever suffered from anxiety or insomnia, you may understand the panic and terror you begin to feel as night falls.

The chain of events happened like this: insomnia –> anxiety –> postpartum depression.

These were the worst of times.

Over time as Sassafras grew, she slept in longer stretches as most babies do, and with the help of medication and therapy, so did I. Over the last fifteen months, our bedtime routine has evolved into something I look forward to at the end of the day. In the early days, it was endless holding, rocking, shushing, and patting until I thought my arms would fall off. When she got a little older, a bath and a warm bottle would usually do the trick, with it not taking very long for her to drift off to sleep. Then once she learned to cruise, she would play for a while and take a few laps around the crib before falling asleep. These days, I usually read her a few favorite books of her choice, and then I sing her a few songs; she follows along with swaying and hand motions and always asks for "more" at the end of each song. At the end of our medley, she'll sit up and point to her crib, I'll ask her if she wants Pooh Bear, and she'll nod. Then I kiss her good night, tell her I love her, and wave bye-bye.

Last night was different. At the end of our songs, Sassafras was quiet and still and I asked her if she wanted Pooh Bear, and she shook her head no. Puzzled, I asked her, "Do you want Umma?" and I pointed to myself. She nodded and smiled, and laid her head on my shoulder. I sat with my girl for some time before reluctantly letting her go, but I could have easily held her tight all night.

I beat Pooh Bear.

These are the best of times.

EXPECTING THE UNEXPECTED

OCTOBER 10, 2012

I am sure we have all heard this phrase now and then. I first heard it while training to go overseas for an "alternative" spring break trip with my church. And through the years, I've learned this is one of those life lessons, a mantra if you will, and not just something to keep in mind in preparation for a big event.

Things rarely go as planned.

We often use the term "expecting" when we are with child. And we make plans. We make plans to make plans. We plan to "try" so we can become expectant parents. Some even make birth plans. And sometimes the plan works out beautifully. And then there are times when it doesn't. Like for the couple who has been trying to get pregnant for three years before medical professionals suggest they seek "other options." Or for the couple whose adoption takes months longer than expected due to unforeseen circumstances, and are forced to jump through one hoop after another before they can be united with their child. Or the couple who cannot carry their baby to full-term, and for the mama who delivers her baby, only to spend a few hours with her child before she leaves this world. Nobody plans for *this*.

I had plans. I had plans to try to get pregnant and have a smooth pregnancy, labor, and delivery. I planned to take my baby home, be exhausted (but not out of my mind), breast-feed my baby the entire first year, or at the very least until I went back to work after a 5.5-month maternity leave, and absolutely love being a mom.

My first pregnancy ended in a miscarriage at 6 weeks. I threw up every day during my second pregnancy until I was 4.5 months pregnant (if you've ever thrown up in a public restroom, staring at those toilets will make you even sicker). At 5 months pregnant, my amniotic fluid levels were dangerously low and I had doctor's orders to stay off my feet, and at 6 months I failed my glucose test and was diagnosed with gestational diabetes. I suffered from postpartum depression, could not nurse beyond 4 weeks (and Sassafras was completely on formula by the time she was 2 months old), and I struggled to find my new identity as a mom. This is not what I expected.

What I am learning on this journey of motherhood is plans go awry. Things do not always go as expected. Babies do not always do what they are "supposed" to – like sleep for 4–5 hour stretches right out of the womb or not have a poop explosion just after you've changed them (or for us lucky ones, in the middle of a diaper change). Some folks do not get pregnant at the drop of a hat (or condom), and our plans go out the window.

And when they do, we learn to let go of control, and even when we feel bruised and battered, we become more real and have a greater ability to really *see* people, and something beautiful happens.

SASSAFRAS'S SLEEP EVOLUTION: NEWBORN TO 15 MONTHS

OCTOBER 17, 2012

As I am looking back on Aliya's eat/sleep journal from her first year, I wonder at what copious notes I took during those first few months. In retrospect, I admit I was a *little* obsessive.

In the first few weeks, there was no real routine or schedule other than feeding her every 2–3 hours. Mind you, that is 2–3 from start to start … so if you start feeding at 11 and your baby takes forever and a day to eat like mine did (about 45 minutes a session), she could be hungry again at 1, giving you just over an hour to sleep or eat or poop or shower. These are little luxuries you take for granted before you have a child.

Truth be told, the newborn schedule sucks.

And being the rule-abiding person I am, even though many seasoned moms (whose babies all lived) told me to let my baby sleep for as long as she could in the middle of the night, my pediatrician said the longest she should go between feedings was 3.5 hours. So I set alarms. And I would wake my baby up to eat. And I basically never slept. And then I went crazy. But that is another story for another time.

In the early weeks, some moms asked me, "So is she on a schedule?" or "Do you have your routine down?" And I would think, "I'm supposed to have her on a schedule?" Usually I would respond with a blank stare or sobs. Sassafras had no semblance of a real schedule until around the 8-week mark when she started to sleep in longer stretches. There was no real nap schedule since she was essentially sleeping in spurts all day long.

Between 10 and 12 weeks, she was *finally* able to stretch out her night-time sleep to a 6-7 hour uninterrupted stretch; once this happened, her day-time naps became much more predictable. By 3 months of age, her awake/sleep times looked something like this:

Wake-up: 6:30 A.M.
Nap 1: 8–9:45 A.M.
Nap 2: 12–2 P.M.
Nap 3: 4–5:30 P.M.
Bed time: 8:30 P.M.
Dreamfeed: 11 P.M.

Sassafras stayed on a 3-nap schedule until she was 8 months old. After weeks of fighting naps and what I call "crap-napping," which consisted of naps about thirty minutes a piece (with about 30–45 minutes of fussing or crying prior to the nap), I figured it might be time to drop a nap. I was a little fearful of the 3-to-2 nap transition, but was pleasantly surprised when she began napping beautifully after the transition! Her crap-napping ceased, and she began taking 1.5–2 hour naps, which I believed to be nothing short of a miracle. Her 2-nap schedule looks something like this:

Wake-up: 7:10 A.M.
Nap 1: 9:45–11:30 A.M.
Nap 2: 2:45–4:45 P.M.
Bed time: 8:15 P.M.

Aliya's nap schedule varies on Sundays since she is in child-care at church during her regular morning nap time. On these days we usually give her one long nap, from 1 to 4 P.M., and we put her down for bed a little earlier, although she usually ends up falling asleep at about the same time. And even though bed time is around 8 P.M., some days she falls asleep quickly, but she often takes a while to wind down, babbling and singing to herself, playing with Pooh Bear, and traipsing around her crib. We are currently experiencing the height of separation anxiety so bed times have been more challenging than normal, but I am hoping this is just a phase.

WHEN THE LIGHTS WENT OUT: POSTPARTUM DEPRESSION

It took me a long time to write about my experience with postpartum depression because it was such a dark time in my life I never wished to revisit. Writing things down has always been a way for me 1) to articulate my experiences and thoughts in a coherent way (when thoughts stay in my head for too long they're either packed away into the abyss of my memory or they become extremely muddled) and 2) to heal.

Postpartum depression (PPD) is one of those terrible, unpredictable, uncontrollable events surrounding pregnancy I never expected to experience after having a baby.

There may have been some things contributing to my "level of risk" in having PPD:

I have a family history of depression (although I did not have a personal history of depression).

I had a higher-than-normal level of anxiety during my pregnancy, as I had gotten pregnant one month after experiencing a miscarriage with my first pregnancy.

I do not deal well with change. I like routines, predictability, and schedules.

I am a bit of a perfectionist. Some might call me an over-achiever.

The first two weeks postpartum were exhausting, but I was in a state of bliss. I am certain my body was running on hormones and adrenaline. I was elated – completely in love with my baby and so grateful she was born healthy and without complications.

Then came week three. And exhausted does not even begin to describe how tired I was. I do not think a word exists in the English language to accurately portray how tired I felt. I learned sleep deprivation has been used as a torture method for prisoners of war; this is probably the closest description of how I was beginning to feel. Tortured. With no way to escape.

I am convinced what began my downward spiral was my **insomnia**. Anxiety breeds insomnia, which further breeds anxiety. It is a fun never-ending cycle. I was hyper-vigilant about Aliya's feeding and sleep times. I counted her poop diapers and pee diapers. I had an overactive flow, which made breastfeeding a stressful time for both mama and baby. When she was asleep, I always worried she would wake up, and when she was awake, I was afraid she would not sleep. So I could not sleep. I had many opportunities to sleep, but my brain refused to shut off. At best, I was sleeping *two hours a day* (meaning two hours in a 24-hour period) for several days straight, and then at some point I began to lose my mind.

Here is a progression of some thoughts I began to have at this time:

I am losing my mind. I do not know how I can do this another day. I am never going to sleep again. How am I supposed to take care of my baby if I never sleep again? My husband is going to leave me because I am losing my mind and I am not the sane woman he married. Then I will have to be a single mom. I am not cut out to be a mother. I am a failure. I am incompetent. I am a terrible mother. I do not know what I am doing. I feel hopeless. I will feel hopeless forever. Perhaps I will be institutionalized.

Any rational person could tell you these are all untrue, but these thoughts and others became scarily true to me, and I felt panicked. All day long. I could no longer keep it all together because I no longer knew how. And my inability to "enjoy every moment" made me feel guiltier by the minute. (As you know, I am convinced that any mother who tells you to "enjoy every minute" is far removed from and has long forgotten the horror of sleep deprivation.)

I felt embarrassed and terrified about PPD. Before having a baby, I was confident. I had always excelled in school, from K-12 all the way through college and graduate school; I had been successful in my career, quickly advancing from one position to the next. I prided myself in being an excellent worker and a fast learner. After having a baby, I felt defeated. Becoming a mom was clearly the hardest thing I have ever had to do; my life as I knew it was forever changed, and being a mother was something I needed to learn by doing.

I knew what I was experiencing was more than just "the blues" and so I sought help very early on. I was desperate. I was desperate to get better not only for my family's sake, but for my own sanity. And I am so glad I did.

Today, I am alive. My baby is alive. Both are amazing feats I was not so sure were possible in the early days. In the early days, I did not know if I was going to make it to tomorrow, much less the next hour.

If you are experiencing PPD, please know you are not alone. PPD is an illness and is treatable. Do not be afraid to ask for help. You will get better.

DAY BY DAY, MOMENT TO MOMENT: COPING WITH POSTPARTUM DEPRESSION

OCTOBER 31, 2012

I am fortunate to have known very early on I was exhibiting many symptoms of postpartum depression. I had several health professionals express concern for me – my pediatrician, one of my nurses whom I met with for a follow-up appointment for my gestational diabetes, a friend of mine who is a labor-and-delivery nurse, and a family member who is a doctor. Initially, when what I thought were just a couple of rough days turned into an inability to fall and stay asleep, anxiety, fear, hopelessness, and uncontrollable crying all day long, I knew it was time to seek professional help.

While I was open to seeking and receiving help, I was **terrified** to go on antidepressants.

I was scared to go on any medication; I had been loading myself with information from internet forums and websites about all of the crazy side effects of antidepressants and horror stories of people coming off of the medication. What I learned is the internet is a free and public space where *many people will share more negative than positive experiences* with depression medication. I also had several friends share with me their experiences using different antidepressants, and friends of friends' experiences on certain medications, warning me not to take certain drugs because they might make me feel even worse.

I am sure the intent of these narratives was to inform and give me some perspective, but I was already feeling panicky and anxious, and all of these warnings scared the living daylights out of me. I had anxiety about my anxiety, anxiety about going on medication, and anxiety about coming off of medication.

The best piece of advice I could give to any mom who is considering going on antidepressants for PPD is to **talk to a medical/health professional**. You can start with your OB to get a prescription, but a psychiatrist will be more informed on each of the different drug choices and side effects, and can monitor/adjust your dosage. My psychiatrist was also able to answer all of my questions and ease my fears about going on medication.

I also felt an extreme amount of guilt. The second key piece to my road to recovery was therapy. I have heard over and over again that often the fastest road to recovery from PPD is medication + therapy. I tried meeting with a couple different therapists, and the one I chose did not accept my insurance. I felt guilty about the cost of therapy; without insurance, many licensed therapists will charge anywhere from $100–200 on average per session and I needed to see someone weekly. I would never have gone without my husband's full support and encouragement. One friend said **the best gift I could give to my family was a healthy self**, and I should not put a price on my health. It was difficult to view my mental health this way; in the end, I knew it was not my "choice" to be depressed and I could not "snap out of it" and this was one essential piece to getting better.

These are some key things I found to be helpful on my road to recovery:

- **GET DRESSED.** My doctor/family member advised me to do this. When I asked her why this was important, she said, "Because that's what normal people do." I could have lived in my lounge pants and nursing tanks with dried breast milk stains for days, but getting dressed actually helped me feel like a normal human being.
- **GET OUT.** As in, GET OUT OF THE HOUSE. I did not realize how important this was for my mental state until I had not left the house for three weeks and began feeling like a prisoner. Get out. Go to Target. Be with other human beings even if it is for a short period of time. A little bit of fresh air and sunlight can help lift your mood.
- **Medication/antidepressants**
- **Therapy**
- **EXERCISE.** Exercise releases endorphins and is known to be a natural mood-lifter.
- **ASK FOR HELP.** I cannot tell you how many family members and friends surrounded me during this difficult time. I had friends who would come by during the day, just to be with me so I would not be alone, or to hold my baby. My mom was over almost every day, before work, after work, and even through the night sometimes. My sister called me every day, sometimes several times a day to check in on me. My sister-in-law would come and take care of the dishes, or our laundry, and would rock Aliya to sleep. Friends brought over meals. I hate asking for help, but I do not know how I would have gotten through my PPD without it.
- **DISTRACTION.** If you can find something to distract yourself or help lighten your mood so you are not fixated on the negative and hopeless thoughts/feelings, do it. I

watched a lot of Korean dramas during my postpartum period! But only the funny ones, and not the ones where someone has a terminal illness and dies. I did not know how I would handle a depressing storyline in my mental state.

- **BOOKS on PPD.** I read a couple of books on postpartum depression. One that I would highly recommend is *This Isn't What I Expected: Overcoming Postpartum Depression.* This book helped me understand what PPD is, informed me on the emotional and physical symptoms of PPD, and offered coping strategies.

- **Other PPD Resources.** www.postpartum.net and www.postpartumprogress.com are wonderful online resources where you can find PPD information, as well as PPD support groups in your area.

My mantra during the early postpartum days was "**day by day.**" Seeing what a struggle it was for me to get through each day, my mom added, "**moment to moment.**" Don't worry about the day, you just need to get through right now. Trying to discipline my mind to focus on the now instead of having anxiety about the unforeseeable future was so helpful. I did not know what the night would bring or what tomorrow would bring, but I knew what was happening right now, right in front of me.

You will have some good days, and you will have some bad days. At the onset of my PPD, they were all bad days. I had not smiled or laughed in weeks, and one day around the 5 or 6-week mark, I had a good day. And I cried. I cried because I feared this would be my only good day for the rest of my life and all the rest would continue to be bad days. But rest assured, as your little one grows, you will have better days and, eventually, your good days will outnumber the bad ones. And the bad days do not mean you are taking a step back; remember to celebrate your good days.

You will get better.

OVERCOMING POSTPARTUM DEPRESSION: A NEW NORMAL

NOVEMBER 8, 2012

If you have ever suffered from depression, whether it was circumstantial or you have a history of depression, you understand how painfully difficult it is just to get through each day. I heard one person describe depression as "hell on earth." Others have shared how depression and anxiety can feel like a never-ending cycle; you become anxious about being anxious, and depressed about being depressed. One of the greatest fears is you will forever feel this way. This was my greatest fear.

At my worst, I believed I would never enjoy life again. My new lot in life was to not have a life; I would be a slave. I would never sleep again, I would never go out again, and I would always feel confused, stumbling through my new role as a mother. I terribly missed my *old* life. I asked a friend of mine when her life began to feel normal again after having her first child. She said five months.

Five months sounded like an eternity when I was living in three-hour cycles. My three-hour world looked something like this:

- Change diaper
- Breastfeed – 45 minutes
- Burp – 5–10 minutes

- Stare at each other (or stare at baby while baby stares at something else) – 30 minutes
- Rock baby to sleep – 20 minutes–1 hour+
- Watch baby sleep – 45 minutes–2 hours
- Repeat cycle

None of this felt *normal*. I wondered how much longer I could survive in my sleep-deprived and depressed state. Previously simple tasks like going out were now an overwhelming ordeal:

Did I pack enough diapers? Do I have enough formula? How many hours will I be out? Will she need one bottle or two? Did I pack her extra outfit? Where's her pacifier? Do I have enough wipes? Should I feed her now or later? Should I take her out right before or right after her nap?

So I just decided to stay home for about five weeks until I went stir crazy.

Friends and family told me it would take time and practice to learn and adjust to being a mom and caring for a newborn. My tendency to want to do things "right" and learn quickly did not serve me well. I realized how extremely "Type A" I am, which was probably more of a shock to me than to anyone who knows me; all this time I thought I was very self-aware. And my mama friends reminded me they had all been there and this was a **new normal**. Imagine that.

My therapist said it this way:

"You will be you, but a better version of you."

I just about fell out of my chair. A better version of me? Postpartum Me seemed to be a much *worse* version of me – a panicked, hopeless, anxious, incompetent Me – someone whom I no longer recognized. Slowly but surely (and *with help*), I embraced my new normal and my new identity as a mom. And I am better.

During an interview, Ellen DeGeneres asked Pink, the singer, how she has changed as a result of being a mom. She said, "I'm way more fun."

It's true. Now you can find me cruising through the aisles at Target talking to my little person or talking to myself. Sometimes we sing our way through the aisles depending on the day. Every morning is a dance party. We laugh about nothing. We take joy in little strolls and holding hands. We make instant friends with strangers. We share inside jokes.

I cannot imagine my life any other way.

It's better. And I'm better. And you will be too.

IT TAKES A VILLAGE

NOVEMBER 26, 2012

Many of us have heard this statement: It takes a village to raise a child.

Few things have been more true of my parenting journey than this.

Our family just celebrated Thanksgiving, and I would say what I am extra thankful for this year is my "village."

My husband: None of this would be possible without him. He is more than my sperm donor and the man who pays the bills; he is my best friend for life. When he isn't working his tail off, you can find him playing with our girl, cooking a gourmet meal, or asking me to spend a night out. He helps me stay grounded when my Type A ways spin mercilessly out of control, and encourages me to dream when I am too afraid to imagine the possibilities. "How do I love thee? Let me count the ways."

Family caregivers: During the work week, my mom and sister-in-law help take care of Sassafras. While I was pregnant, KK and I had already planned to put Sassafras into daycare at the end of my maternity leave, but due to a combination of circumstances my mom made the decision to retire a few years early to help me with Sassafras when I went back to work. She has been a godsend for our family and for my girl. I am always amazed at her energy and the joy she has in spending her days with Sassafras. While my mom watches her four weekdays, my sister-in-law watches her one day a week, and as a bonus helps with Sassafras as needed and gives KK and me the occasional date night out. Having the blessing of family available to help care for our baby eased my transition from maternity leave back into full-time work at the office. There is nothing quite like it. I am convinced part of the reason why Aliya is such a happy girl is because of the love and care she receives from so many of us.

Friends: Several friends carried me through my postpartum period. Motherhood can be very lonely and isolating at times, particularly when you are feeling confused and exhausted and have no idea what you are doing. Some friends volunteered to come by the house when they knew I was going to be alone and I would be having an especially difficult time; one friend even rearranged childcare plans for her two kids to come and help me for a few mornings. Nowadays they give me relief and help me relax; they help me remember who I was prior to having Sassafras and who I am now. They can be brutally honest about the ups and downs of life in whatever season or stage of life, whether they are single, dating, or married, and have one kid, two kids, three kids, or no kids (I left out four+ kids because in my mind, you are all other-worldly with supernatural powers). Aliya is lucky to have so many aunties and uncles.

Work: I may be in the minority, but I love the work I do and the people with whom I work. They were brimming with excitement for me while I was pregnant, threw a lavish baby shower for me, were generous with my maternity leave, and were so supportive when I returned. This has made all the difference in my decision to return to work and be a full-time working mom. While I miss Sassafras throughout the day, I enjoy my work and my work family. If I worked anywhere else, I might feel differently.

So, thank you, Village. I hope everyone had a wonderful Thanksgiving.

MORE THAN . . .

DECEMBER 7, 2012

Parenthood can be more than you ever imagined it to be.

It can be more trying, challenging, humbling, taxing, exhausting, and heartbreaking than you ever thought possible.

The sleepless nights may feel torturous. Or perhaps you had to be separated from your child while they spent many nights, weeks, or months in the hospital and each minute away from your baby tore you apart. Or maybe your child's endless whining, crying, and screaming is wearing on your last nerve. Children have a way of terrorizing capable, functioning adults.

And I have not even reached "the terribles" or the teenage years yet.

But for as many tough moments you may experience as a parent, there is an infinite number of joy-filled moments. Parenthood can be more healing, heartwarming, joyful, and amazing than you ever imagined. I often stare at Sassafras and wonder, "How did we become so blessed to call you ours?" Children have a way of tugging at your heartstrings and melting you to pieces.

I am constantly reminding myself there will be good days and bad days; there will be some sleepless nights and there will be glorious nights; there will be outrageous tantrums and outbursts and there will be impromptu laugh attacks and dance parties; she will test me and she will love me.

She makes this incredible journey all worth it.

YOU ARE DOING JUST FINE

DECEMBER 17, 2012

There are days when motherhood can feel like a battlefield. To date, it is by far the hardest "job" I have ever done, one where the hours are 24/7 and training manuals do not quite do the trick. You must learn as you go, the stakes are high, and just when you feel you have mastered one thing, everything changes. With each stage, one thing gets easier and another gets harder. This does not always bode well for perfectionist worrywarts like myself.

In the early days, I remember often feeling like I was failing miserably. I had difficulty breastfeeding and, with the onset of my postpartum depression, could not find the wherewithal to continue trying. I felt overwhelmed with exhaustion and the newness of it all, and felt like an imposter since about 99% of the time I had no idea what I was doing.

It seemed simple enough in my head before she was born: you change them, feed them, burp them, play with them, and rock them to sleep. And as they get older, you play and interact with them a little more, but the general formula stays the same. At some point you throw discipline and potty training into the mix, and overall you let them know just how much you love them.

Then she was born and I realized moms have the toughest job in the world.

During a difficult transition into motherhood, I was fortunate to have some veteran moms rally around me. They would say, "You are doing just fine!" I wondered how I had not been found out yet, but they said, "She's eating, sleeping, and growing. What else is a baby to do?" They reminded me they had all been in the same place before, and encouraged me to face things one day at a time.

Day by day ...

We are on the 12th day of what we think is a stomach virus that has been ailing Sassafras (and recently hit our entire household). In these last two weeks, I revisited some of the thoughts and feelings from the early days. We have had several sleepless nights, about a hundred loads of laundry, and doctor visits, all of which have resulted in fatigue, frustration, and feelings of helplessness. Somehow, Aliya has managed to keep a smile on her face; I threw up for one day and was an anxious, crying mess. Who is the baby here?

And so even after these 12 days, I have to remind myself ... we are doing just fine. Day by day.

Moms also have the best job in the world.

18 MONTHS

DECEMBER 26, 2012

Sassafras is 18 months. I was shocked and amazed by the amount of development that happens in the first year, but each day I feel like she continues to change at warp speed, learning new words and mimicking me (for better or for worse). One day out of the blue, she started shaking her finger at me saying, "No no!" And just this past week she said, "Wait" – long and drawn out with her hand palm out like me. Now when she says "bye" to her dolls, she gives them each a hug and kiss, just the way I do when I am saying bye to her in the mornings when I leave for work. I need to watch myself around this girl.

Sleeping: We are still attempting two naps a day, but some days when Aliya wakes up later, around 7:30 A.M., she skips her first nap altogether and just takes one long afternoon nap for about 3–3.5 hours. We usually take this day by day, but I think in the next few weeks we will transition her over to one nap. She seems to be gradually making this transition on her own. She still takes a paci for her naps, but we weaned her of her nighttime paci when she turned one. For the most part, she has always been a good sleeper except for when teething or sickness is involved – then all bets are off.

Teeth: Aliya has 6.5 teeth (the 7th tooth is not full grown yet) and is currently cutting 3 teeth (possibly more) from what I can see. She was 9 months old before she cut her very first tooth, and now it seems like they are all just coming in at once. These days, she is a drooly mess.

Language: I have lost track of Sassafras's word count. She can say many dual-syllable words, and will try to repeat whatever you say, although much of the time it comes out as gibberish. For example, she pronounces "snowman" as "no-me" and "orange" as "oh-ray." She still uses sign language to supplement frequently used words/phrases, such as milk, please, more, and all done. She still cannot put two words together; if you ask her to say, "Hi Mommy," she will just say the first word.

Personality: She is a ham. She loves to be around people and warms up to new people fairly quickly. She makes friends wherever we go, smiling and saying hi. She laughs easily, at herself and with others. She is very expressive and will try to mimic just about any facial expression you throw her way. She has already learned how to sweet talk when she wants something. I sometimes wonder, "Where on earth did you come from?" She makes me laugh every day.

Motor skills: Aliya started walking at 13 months, and has yet to start running – which is fine by me! Sometimes when we are walking on a decline she will pick up speed, but that is about it. She does not jump, but she will stomp her feet and shrug her shoulders like she's caught air. She has a great throw, and I can already see KK's wheels spinning about which sport to have her try first.

Eating: Ever since she's been on solid foods, she has been an excellent eater. She now eats just about everything we eat, except for desserts, which I will usually eat after she goes to sleep (otherwise I would resort to enjoying it in the pantry or garage); thankfully, she has no known food allergies. Sometimes we worry we are feeding her too much, but her weight has always been right around the 50th percentile. I am not sure where all her food goes; she seems to be a bottomless pit with an ever-expanding belly in the center of her skinny arms and legs. She is a walking belly. I know friends who have difficulty getting their kids to eat anything, so I suppose this is not a terrible problem to have. These days she will try to spoon-feed herself, but after a few failed attempts she will use her hands to shovel every last crumb or grain of rice into her mouth. Sometimes she will lick the plate. Then she will clamor for more.

My little family is the greatest gift to me this Christmas. Before I know it, Aliya will be turning two, and I will cry again, asking God to slow down time. But then I will remember what many mothers have told me before, which is there is much to look forward to, and the best is yet to come. I will try to give myself grace, as I remind myself with each stage, everything is new and I will inevitably stumble along the way. Happy 18 months, baby girl.

THE MOMMY WARS: MOTHERHOOD AND OTHER MOMS

JANUARY 15, 2013

Every mom is different. Every baby is different. And each family's situation is different.

Our varying situations, life experiences, personal family histories, beliefs, values, parenting philosophies, passions, personalities, education, etc. will inevitably shape the way we parent our children and build our families. I am of the mindset what works for one baby/parent/mother/family may not work for another. This is also why I abhor the "mommy wars."

Working moms vs. stay-at-home moms. Breastfeeding vs. formula-feeding. Disposable diapering vs. cloth diapering. Purees vs. baby-led weaning. Cry-it-out (CIO) methods vs. attachment parenting. Natural births vs. the epidural. The list is endless.

Just to give you a bit of background: I am a full-time working mom. The only "birth plan" I had was to get the epidural as soon as I was allowed. I tried to breastfeed (I had every intention to try to do so until my daughter turned one, or at the very least until the end of my maternity leave at around the six-month mark), but by two months my daughter was exclusively on formula. We use disposable diapers, and we did a modified version of CIO when we sleep-trained Aliya at five-and-a-half months.

I have many friends who are stay-at-home moms. Some of my working mama friends wish they could stay at home, but are not able to because they need to have a dual income. I have other stay-at-home mama friends who wish they could work, but financially it makes more sense to stay at home than to pay the hundreds/thousands needed to cover day-care expenses. I have friends who are strong proponents of sleep-training; others who have never sleep-trained and prefer to co-sleep. Every mama is different.

I have been fortunate enough to be surrounded by mothers who are supportive of one another, whether we work or stay at home, breastfeed or formula-feed, sleep-train or co-sleep. Ironically, the one time I felt judged by another parent was in the world of social media, when a father made a comment about those who allow their children to cry-it-out and how they all must be masochistic, selfish, evil human beings (I will refrain from stating verbatim the vulgarities he used in *this* space). There was also another time (before I had children) when someone once informed me I would definitely decide to stay at home if I wanted to do what was best for my family. Well, I never ...

In my experience, it seems the mommy wars have been perpetuated by the media and internet forums (where it is quite easy to pass judgment and say whatever to whomever with no real consideration for a person's situation or feelings), and less by real-life moms I have met. In fact, I have found being a mom has allowed me to make more connections with new people I meet, and it is less polarizing than I had imagined it would be. I could run into another mom in the market, or at church, or in the infant section at Target and all it takes is a "How old is your little one?" to make an instant connection.

Being a parent is hard enough without having someone else tell you all the things you are doing "wrong" as a mother. The way I see it, **as mothers we are in the trenches together**, and are doing the best we can to raise our little ones in the best way possible.

19 MONTHS

JANUARY 30, 2013

Here we are already at the 19-month mark. As Quincy on *Little Einsteins* (of which I have become a frequent watcher these days) always says, "I cannot believe it!"

We had to delay Aliya's 18-month check-up to 19 months because she has been sick since early December. Fourteen days of diarrhea, then roseola, a bilateral ear infection, and a yeast infection. 'Tis the season, but the poor kid has been through the wringer. I am happy to report she is healthy (today)! Her 18 (19)-month stats are 88th percentile for height (33 inches) and 50th percentile for weight (23.2 lbs.).

At this point in time, I have lost track of a number of things.

I do not know her word count. When our pediatrician asked how many words she can say, I guessed 50, but the truth is I lost count after 25. I do know she learns a new word just about every other day, and tries to repeat whatever we say.

I do not know how many teeth she has. A bunch of front ones, and at least one molar fully in with a few others cutting through.

I do not know how much she drinks during the day. I used to meticulously keep track of the exact number of ounces she was drinking (or not drinking) during the day, and coax her to drink more if she did not reach a magic number. Now, I just know she drinks "enough."

I would like to think this is a sign I am easing into mother-hood and I have finally put my constant first-time-mom worries to rest. Or perhaps it means I have just become too exhausted to keep track.

One thing she has become more fascinated with these days is diaper changes. Usually just before or after she has a dirty diaper, she tries to change Pooh Bear's diaper.

Sleep: We finally made the 2-to-1 nap transition! I have been dreading the transition for quite some time. I was afraid keeping her up longer would result in an extra cranky baby in the mornings, selfishly I liked having two "breaks" in the day, and I was not sure how well she would sleep. She was already taking one nap on Sundays since we attend church during her usual first nap time, so the transition has been very smooth. She seems to be sleeping even better during the day (anywhere from 3–3.5 hours) and I have noticed she is able to fall asleep a tad earlier for bed time.

Personality: As she grows, she continues to become more interactive and playful. She loves to mimic, sing songs, and play. She loves to make you laugh, and she laughs at herself quite easily. On the flip side, if she sees someone crying or in pain, she immediately makes a sad face and shows concern. She loves people. To say she is a happy baby is an understatement.

Screen time: In the last month, we began to let Sassafras watch television. I understand screen time can be a bit of a hot button with some moms, but we do allow a little screen time (iPad/iPhone educational apps and some television) at the beginning and end of each day. I know *they* say to wait until children are 2 years old, but I threw in the towel during her marathon month of sickness. There was only so much I could do to comfort her, and *Little Einsteins* brought a little bit of relief and joy to my girl's face. So I gave in.

It has been a chaotic month of travel, holiday gatherings, sickness, ER visits, and sleep deprivation but we made it! I hope to have a grade A health report at 20 months.

A WORKING MAMA'S TALE: THE BLUR

FEBRUARY 14, 2013

As a working mom, I live for my weekends. Weekends are when I get to maximize my time with my family. They are not quite as relaxing as they were pre-parenthood (the days of sleeping in are far behind me), but I cherish the time we get to spend together.

Before I became a mom, I was anxious about how I might handle "the juggle" between my career and my family. I always knew I was more likely to be a working mom than a stay-at-home mom for a variety of reasons. While I was open to the possibility I might want to stay at home after Aliya was born, I always envisioned myself working and having a family. My mom was a prime example for me. For over 25 years she worked over 40 hours a week, sometimes working two jobs when we were younger. And somehow she managed to cart me from one lesson to another, driving from work to school to home to my rehearsals, all without a single complaint. Then there were my friends who are working moms. I remember having lunch with an old colleague of mine who shared that as a working mom, she never felt like she was giving 100% to any one thing. When she was working, she missed her child; when she needed to miss work to be with her child, she felt guilty. I suppose every one of us experiences "mama guilt" from time to time, and it looks different for each of us.

Towards the end of my maternity leave, I sometimes questioned my decision to return to work – not because I did not want to work, but because I wondered if returning to work meant that I did not love my baby enough to stay home. The doubts were self-imposed, and I am fortunate to have a husband, family, and friends who would have supported whatever decision I made.

It has now been over a year since I went back to work full-time after having my baby.

As a mom, I am learning there will be good days and there will be bad days. On a typical day I go to work, I rush home and it is a mad dash to get dinner ready, feed Aliya, play, give her a bath, and begin her bedtime routine. Once she is down for the night, there is always cleaning to do (toys, dishes, floors, etc.), and then sometimes I am back to work, checking and answering emails. If I am feeling extra productive I will shower, and then sleep around midnight, only to do it all over again the next day. A fellow working mama friend calls this "the blur." And lately my life has felt blurry.

Perfectionist tendencies (oh who am I kidding – PERFECTIONISM) have/has not served me well in the course of my life. That "mama guilt" I mentioned before? Mama guilt is not my friend, and yet it is a close companion, often in my head telling me I should be doing more. I should be an excellent wife, mother, sister, daughter, friend, and employee all the time. And I should *always* know what I am doing and *never* make mistakes.

Now that you all know this about me, I will share that becoming a mother has been, and continues to be, one of the most humbling experiences in my life.

And in this blurry season, I have decided to follow the mantra of one of my favorite authors, Shauna Niequist, which is to be **"present over perfect."**

After all, the sooner my daughter realizes I am not perfect, the better off she'll be.

ON THE DAWN OF THE TERRIFIC TWOS

MARCH 8, 2013

Sassafras is now TWENTY months old and we are closely approaching the **Terrific Twos** (which I hear are lackluster compared to the Thrilling Threes). Some days I feel like she is a one-and-a-half-year-old going on thirteen, and I know I will just eat my words once she enters her teenage years. What do parents of teens call those years, I wonder?

These days, Sassafras loves being outside (the upside of warm California winters) so I try to take her out as much as I can on the weekends when I get to spend the most time with her. February was a month of holidays (the upside of working for the government), so we were able to have a few more outings than usual.

One of the local parks nearby houses a small zoo with owls, bears, mountain lions, and a petting zoo; the best part is it is only two dollars for admission!

We also took her to the beach for the first time. We live only fifteen minutes away, but we do not take advantage of this enough. We were hoping for an impromptu picnic lunch on the beach, but the sand and water were too tempting for Aliya and our food too tempting for the psychotic seagulls, so we just let her frolic around instead.

On most weekends, we frequent the park since we have so many close by (we have three in walking distance, one around the corner from our house) and she loves it. She can go down the slide all by herself now, and she beams with pride every time.

When we are not out and about, running around and burning off as much energy as possible, we spend time trying to teach her letters, numbers, shapes, and colors. She now knows her letters (although U and V can be confusing), some numbers, shapes are hit or miss, and I am not sure she understands the concept of colors just yet.

Development: She has been picking up words and phrases at a rapid pace, and can now string a couple words together at a time (e.g., sit down, water all done, oh no, Mommy bye bye, Aliya sleep, Aliya play). She continues to mimic us and our daily activities in her play, and so we watch her put her dolls in her stroller, pretend to eat, pretend to sleep, change her dolls' diapers, and pray with them.

Temperament/Personality: I could not have asked for a happier child. She smiles often and loves people, especially the little ones her size. The older she gets the more *spirited* she becomes. She is both sweet and sassy, sugar and fire. Fortunately, for now, her fiery moments are short-lived and are usually linked to being hungry, bored, or tired; as long as we can curb those three things, she is generally in good spirits.

I thought the first year whizzed by, but it seems the second year is going by even faster. My heart both aches and swells every time I look at my daughter's face. I suppose this is the space we live in as mothers – the tension between holding on and letting go.

FEAR OF THE KNOWN

APRIL 4, 2013

I have struggled to write this for some time. I was afraid revisiting my thoughts on and memories of postpartum depression might cause more anxiety as we talk about possibly expanding our family in the future.

I am more scared today of having a(nother) child than I was two years ago before Aliya was born.

Before Sassafras was born, I feared the unknown. I had no idea what to expect. I was afraid of being an unfit mother, of being able to survive on little to no sleep, on failing at everything. And much to my chagrin, I believed all of these fears had come true when she was born. I am not sure how much the chemical/hormonal imbalance affected my mind, or how much was due to my Type A and self-critical nature. My feelings of guilt, worthlessness, and failure, coupled with insomnia and anxiety, ultimately led me down a dark path of despair and depression; I felt like an impostor, completely helpless and out of control, and was the most scared I had ever felt in my life.

Today, I fear the known.

Moms always say, "You'll forget!" Or better yet, some moms used to say to me, "You'll miss this!"

Perhaps I am not far enough removed to miss it because I have not forgotten and still remember the painful details of that time.

I have forgotten things like when she learned how to sit up. Or when she rolled over for the first time. Or how many ounces she was drinking at 4 months. Luckily I have thousands of photos and fewer blog entries documenting these milestones. Yes, I am *that* mom – the one who litters your Facebook Newsfeed with hour-by-hour updates.

I have not forgotten the sleepless nights. Or how Aliya would cry and scream during feedings and how defeated I felt when I made the decision to put her exclusively on formula at 8 weeks. Or feeling completely alone. Or wondering when KK would realize I had completely lost my mind. Even though I was in a fog, I still remember *all of it*.

Who knew having a newborn could be so terrifying?

I am sure part of my experience had to do with the anxiety every first-time mom has with her first baby. And while I know I will never be a first-time mom again, I also know there is a very real possibility I may experience postpartum depression again.

I may just be insane enough to do it all over again. I just need to finish writing my pros and cons list.

21 MONTHS

APRIL 8, 2013

21 months. I think I have been putting off plans for Sassafras's 2nd birthday party because I am partly in denial. Most days I cannot believe she is almost two years old. In my last monthly update, I shared about her fiery moments, which are becoming more frequent but are thankfully still short-lived.

She is one busy little girl! The biggest milestone this month is language. In just a few short weeks, she has gone through a language explosion of sorts, saying more and more words together, learning new words, and singing whole songs. Her favorite songs right now are Jesus Loves Me, ABCs, and a few Korean children's songs. She mimics *everything* – actions, expressions, and words. She continues to reenact her daily activities with her dolls, and also share her activities with them. When she dances or eats, Pooh Bear must be present. Pooh Bear is her dancing partner, dining buddy, lovey, and maybe even her best friend for life.

She is beginning to outgrow all of her 18 and 18–24 month clothes, and we are now officially out of hand-me-downs. Since birth, I have had bags and bags of used clothes from generous mama friends; I thought I had an endless supply and now here we are at the end! Girl clothes are so cute and they grow out of them so fast. I am hoping now that we have hit 2T sizes, she will be able to wear her clothes a bit longer. Luckily Target, Old Navy, H&M, and babyGAP have so many great and affordable finds on sale. She cannot quite get herself dressed yet, but she has started to try putting on her socks and shoes. So far she cannot get them past her big toes.

She also started wearing everyone's shoes for size and will try to walk around the house with them.

She continues to eat and sleep well, and after a dreadful December and January, I am happy to share healthy reports for March and April. It makes a *world* of difference when your baby is feeling well. I will try to remember the healthy months when we start her in daycare in the summer.

She is becoming a little girl right before my very eyes. Her big personality just kills me, and I so wish I could just put my fingers together and freeze time.

A WORKING MAMA'S TALE: THE WORK-LIFE BALANCE

MAY 3, 2013

Over the last couple of months, I have made an effort to attend networking lunches and reach out to other successful working mothers to hear about their experiences as female leaders, and as working moms.

In all honesty, I have just been wanting to hear from other more seasoned working moms that it is entirely possible to 1) be a great worker and 2) be a great mother. While I acknowledge work can and often does provide a much needed "break" in the day, it does not keep me from missing my daughter each and every day. On the flip side, I know I would not have as many opportunities to miss her as a stay-at-home mom, and knowing myself I would probably be clamoring to get back to the office. As mothers, we are all in the trenches and nothing is ever easy.

At our last networking lunch, one of the female leaders on campus who has had a lucrative career and held executive high-level positions for Fortune 500 companies in the private sector was invited to speak to a group of about fifty women. You could just feel the energy and enthusiasm from all of the women in the audience. She made it a point to share briefly about her children and her experience as a working mom, and had we been in a more informal setting chatting over coffee, I would have asked her about twenty questions: "What's your secret? How did you do it? If you had to do it all over again, would you be a working mom?" And the million-dollar question: **"How do you handle the work-life balance?"**

But I just asked her one:

"My working mom friends have shared that they never feel like they are giving 100% to any one area of their lives (work vs. family). Would you agree?"

And she went on to share a bit more background about her work and her family, some suggestions for working moms, and an anecdote. She was always there for her kids' scheduled meetings and events: sports games, awards nights, concerts, parent-teacher conferences, etc. Even with her busy schedule, she never missed a single event. What she did miss were all of the *unscheduled* moments: being there when her kids fell down; witnessing all of their milestones first-hand; taking them out to movies after school; collecting sand on the beach for a school project.

She cried. And I cried.

How unprofessional.

What I have gathered from these women are some suggestions I hope will be helpful for other working moms:

Support system: If you are going to be successful at work, you need a strong support system. For many (myself included), their primary support comes from their spouse/partner/significant other. I can confidently say I would not be where I am in my career without my husband's support and encouragement. When there are evening or weekends I am required to work, he will play single daddy for the day without hassle or complaint (and vice versa). There are many others in my "village" who make up this support system and give me confidence as a working mom each day.

Childcare: You need to have a good childcare system in place, one you have confidence in, and caregivers with whom you feel comfortable leaving your child during the day. I have been extremely fortunate to have my family around to watch Sassafras these last two years.

Draw boundaries: Leave your work at work. I will be the first to admit I am *terrible* at this. My first mistake was connecting my work email to my iPhone so I could always be connected. What I must remind myself is nothing needs to be answered at 10 P.M. The work will still be there when I arrive at the office in the morning. Evenings and weekends are for my family, and I want to be fully present when I am at home.

Self-care: As mothers, it is our natural inclination to put everyone else's needs before our own. And as a working mom, when I come home after a full day of work, I am in a rush to get dinner on the table, give Sassafras a bath, play, begin her bedtime routine, clean the house, and rest before I do it all over again the next day. By 9 or 10 P.M., I want to do nothing. And so I let my body atrophy whilst snacking and watching trashy reality television shows or playing games on my phone. This is another area in which I would like to grow – in taking better care of myself, spending time in life-giving friendships, and doing things that energize rather than deplete me.

Be proud of your work/Love what you do: This is more of a luxury than a necessity/tip/recommendation, but it does help to love what you do at work. I am proud of the work I do, and this helps fuel me to continue doing what I do.

A WORKING MAMA'S TALE: TODDLER PLAY DATES

MAY 16, 2013

One thing I hugely miss about staying at home (while on maternity leave) is having regular play dates. Not being able to have regular play dates makes me sad on two accounts: 1) Sassafras does not have a group of friends she sees regularly throughout the week since she stays at home with my family; 2) by way of Number One, I also do not have a group of mom friends I see regularly throughout the week. Scheduling play dates on weekends can sometimes be a challenge since for many families (including my own), weekends are often set aside for special family time since it is really the only extensive amount of time during the week you have altogether.

Perhaps in some idyllic corner of my mind, I imagine stay-at-home moms pouring their hearts out over a cup of coffee while their sweet children run around, laugh, and play. In reality, I know a majority of the time together may actually be spent on discipline, teaching, feeding, and making sure the kids do not rip each other to shreds or self-destruct. But seeing Aliya interact with other children her age and having time to **connect** with other moms make my heart happy. Since this is important me, I have tried to be somewhat creative in my approach of organizing play dates.

Holidays/Administrative closures/Vacation: Since I work in the public sector, I take full advantage of my days off! Sassafras recently had a blast playing with her friend (they are seven weeks apart in age) at the park. We headed to the playground around 10:45 A.M., had lunch together, and got home just in time for her afternoon nap.

Early-evening play dates: My normal work hours are from 7:30 A.M. to 4:30 P.M., so on most days I manage to get home close to 5 P.M. My husband occasionally works evenings, so I try to plan my after-work play dates on nights when he is already out of the house so that I am not depriving him of daddy-daughter time. My friends and I take turns providing a kid-friendly dinner, or sometimes we will make it a potluck to ease the burden (or share the joy) of cooking.

I am extremely fortunate to have a number of friends nearby who are moms with children close to Sassafras's age, many of whom I have known since college – pre-marriage, pre-baby, pre-life-as-we-know-it. I am grateful to be able to walk through this journey of motherhood with them.

A LETTER TO MY TWO-YEAR-OLD DAUGHTER

JUNE 26, 2013

You're TWO. We keep telling you you're two, and you keep saying, "I'm ONE." It looks as though that defiant spirit is innate. We'll have to work on that.

You, my daughter, are my favorite little person in the whole world. You are the best part of my day. Seeing you learning, growing, and happy brings me so much joy. I'm learning how to see the world again for the first time through your eyes.

Let's begin with the things you love.

You love family. You've had four different caregivers in your short lifetime – me, Daddy, halmoni (that would be your grandmother), and gomoh (your Aunt Colleen). Daddy's convinced that you are learning at lightning speed because you are surrounded by so many who love you.

You love your friends. You give hugs and you light up when you see them. Your best friends right now are Luke, Abby, and Isla.

You love Winnie the Pooh. And the whole gang.

You love puppies. And babies. Basically, all things miniature.

You love avocados. And ice cream. And noodles.

You love fountains and giant bodies of water.

You love to sing and dance. Everything becomes a song or a dance party.

You hate the swings. You're cautious. And most of the time you're willing to try anything once, as long as you know we will be there to catch you.

You hate broccoli. I think we may have traumatized you by not seasoning it when you first had it. Oops.

You hate to be restrained. You want to do things when you want to do them. But perhaps this is all two-year-olds.

You hate when I leave the room. I'm trying to relish this for as long as possible because I know there will be a day when you would love nothing more than to not be in a room with me. If that ever happens, it just means I'm being a good mom.

This second year of life has gone by much too fast. In the last year you learned how to walk, you learned the alphabet and numbers one through ten; you began to play much more with your doll toys (changing their imaginary diapers) and play food (pretending to cook and eat). You know the words to Jesus Loves Me, God is So Good, Wheels on the Bus, Happy Birthday, and a fair share of Korean children's songs.

Your favorite things to say right now are "Aliya funny!" and "Aliya do it" and "Umma shoulder" (when you want me to hold you) and "No time-out."

You love to snuggle and cuddle with me when I'm doing something (like cooking or changing clothes), but when it's time to cuddle before bed time you won't have any of it.

When someone is sad, you immediately notice and show concern. I can tell that even at two, you have a big heart.

Today I took the day off because I simply wanted to be with you and I know how much you love to be with me. We went to the park to play and see your friends, and then the pool. We ate some of your favorite things, and because you made it very clear that you wanted some "happy birthday cake" I baked you my personal favorite – Funfetti cake with rainbow chip frosting. I'm sorry baby, but it will be a new day if I ever bake you anything from scratch. I didn't get the cooking/baking gene.

I'm looking forward to this next year. People always talk about the terrible twos, but how terrible could they be? Maybe you will find out next year when I write your 3rd birthday letter.

I love you, Aliya. I love being your mom. You have been the greatest gift to me, and every day I want to be better because of you. Happy 2nd birthday, sweetheart.

Love,
Umma

ALIYA TURNS 2

JUNE 26, 2013

Aliya is now two years old. I am the mother of a two-year-old.

This means 1) we have survived two years of parenthood and 2) our child has survived two years of our parenting.

Aliya's second year of life (and our second year as parents) has felt vastly different from Year One. Year One, particularly the first couple months, had its share of challenges. Kevin had just begun his new post as an assistant principal, and he had a very shell-shocked, depressed wife and new mom at home. We had absolutely no idea what we were doing. Does anyone, really, when they have just brought a tiny six-pound human being home for the first time? Whoever said taking care of puppies was adequate training for those aspiring to become parents probably never had children.

But Year One came and went. All the while, baby grew and grew, and was healthy and as happy as can be. Once she learned how to smile, she never stopped, and neither did I. It took her about seven weeks to learn how to do it, but once she figured out how to turn up the corners of her mouth, I made it my mission in life to capture every smile and funny face for all of my social media outlets because who wouldn't want to see a picture of my kid? Maybe now that she is two, I'll refrain from posting a daily photo online with the caption, "BEST KID EVER."

What can I say? I'm in love.

They (and by "they," I mean my therapist) say it takes time to build a relationship. In the early days, I could not think straight. Not sleeping will do that to you. I would stare at her and just think, "I don't care what you do in life. Just sleep. Please sleep. Nothing would make me happier or prouder than a five-hour stretch of sleep." And eventually she did. And we were able to begin growing that relationship they talk about.

When Aliya turned one, I cried in the last weeks leading up to her birthday because I was sad that my baby wasn't such a baby anymore. But I remember a good friend of mine telling me there was much to look forward to, and there would be even more joy, more laughter, much more to come.

Year Two has come and gone. I have feared the Terrible Twos since before I was even with child, and though Aliya has become more willful and challenging at times, she has also become so deliciously sweet, incredibly affectionate, hilarious, nurturing, charming, and a master imitator. If you ever want to become painfully aware of the things you do and say throughout the day, live with a two-year-old.

Every now and then, she'll really impress me. Tonight, for example, we asked her to choose, "Do you want to play with your piano, or watch your show?" Her response: "Yes. Pia-show." Brilliant, kid, but no dice. Seriously, where does she come up with this stuff?

Unlike last year, I did not cry these past few weeks. I have been *slightly* more excited (and less sad) to celebrate my little girl growing up. We invited all of her friends, and she was so happy to see them and play and eat cake since these, of course, are all the elements of a great birthday party: friends, play, and cake. Today when we told her it was her actual birthday, she began singing the Happy Birthday song and then kept saying, "Aliya's Birthday? Happy Birthday cake!"

We shared the perfect day together (not without its share of tantrums and time-outs), eating and doing all of her favorite things. Happy 2nd Birthday, dear Sassafras. I hope you always know how much you make Mommy's and Daddy's hearts explode. Thank you for turning everything into a song or dance party. You rock.

MAKING MOMMY FRIENDS

AUGUST 19, 2013

Motherhood can be rather isolating at times. In the early months when you are first adjusting to your new identity as a mom (and particularly when your little one is sleeping in spurts and eating around the clock), it is easy to feel alone and lost. I recall during the early days after Sassafras was born, I felt most alone in the wee hours of the night. I wondered when I would fall into step and feel comfortable in my new skin as a mother. Surely I was not the *only* first-time mom who felt this way ... right? I found myself desperate to talk to someone, just about *anyone*, who had children and could reassure me that this motherhood gig was pretty fantastic after all.

The beauty of it all is that every mom has been there. While motherhood can be isolating, motherhood can also bring people together with ease. Becoming a mother is like entering into a sisterhood of women who have experienced their fair share of torturous hazing rituals that include (and are not limited to) episiotomies, bloody nipples, 20+ hours of labor, insomnia/sleep deprivation, 9 months of vomiting, colic, being pooped/peed/vomited on, etc. Strangers share and swap stories about sore leaky boobs or diaper rashes, and all of a sudden there is a connection. Beautiful, isn't it?

I am lucky to have a number of long-time friends with kids around Aliya's age nearby, but I also love meeting new moms and making connections. I will share a couple of tips/ resources that have worked wonderfully for me:

The internet: can be a wonderful way to connect with other moms! Hellobee.com is one example of many fantastic parenting resources out there. Hellobee, as well as other sites like TheBump.com and Babycenter.com, hosts message boards for the community, and some have birth club forums you can join to dialogue with other moms who are due in the same month as you. I met a fantastic group of supportive moms through my birth club, and two years later we still regularly check in with one another, ask questions, and share milestones/victories. Other sites, like meetup.com, may be another way to meet other moms in your area.

Church/Religious organizations: Another avenue by which I have met new moms is through church. Many parents (with young children) attend the earlier Sunday morning service since it fits in quite well with nap times! One Sunday, I happened to be sitting next a couple with a baby about the same age as ours, and the next thing you know we are talking about maternity leave, teething, beginning solid foods, etc. There was an easy, natural connection, and now we have become good friends. Many churches also facilitate groups/meetings specifically for moms to meet, connect, and journey together.

Local park/Indoor play area/Community (swim/music/ art) classes: If you have a neighborhood park nearby, you often see the same parents and children come out to play at roughly the same times each day. My mom watches Sassafras during the day and takes her to the park in the mornings; when I started taking her more regularly in the evenings after work, I was surprised by how many other parents and kids knew my girl! I have gotten to know a few of their names and children as well, and it is nice to see familiar, friendly faces at the park every day.

Sometimes your child may make friends for you, and making mommy friends may be easier than you think! Many moms are seeking to connect with other moms; we all need help, encouragement, and support along this journey.

SUMMER WEDDINGS: TIPS FOR PARENTS

AUGUST 27, 2013

This summer, our family was able to witness and participate in the nuptials of a few very dear friends.

KK was a groomsman for one of the weddings, and Sassafras was a flower girl in the other. I felt so honored that my friend would want our little girl to be a part of her special day, and I asked the bride several times if she was absolutely certain she wanted my Sassafras to participate. She had never been to a wedding prior to this summer, and I was not sure she would be able to sit through the ceremony, much less walk a straight line down the aisle.

If you like predictability, schedules, and a routine, then attending and participating in weddings with a small child can be cause for a little stress for parents. I wanted to make sure 1) Aliya was well-rested and 2) she did not disrupt (i.e., wreak havoc on) the events of the day. Number One can be tricky since we all know the world does not revolve around our children, and neither do wedding ceremonies. Many ceremonies are scheduled right during nap times, and Number Two can be hard to come by if Number One does not happen.

Fortunately, Sassafras had a blast at the two weddings she attended this summer; we attended a third "adults only" wedding without her, which was a blast for an entirely different set of reasons.

Here are some tips I have gathered from these last few weddings:

Be flexible/creative with nap/bed times: When Sassafras was a flower girl for our friend's wedding, she did not take a regular nap on either the rehearsal day or the day of the wedding. I had envisioned her bursting into flames or screaming her way down the aisle, but she surprised us all and did quite well. Perhaps it was all of the excitement (or delirium), but even through her tiredness she enjoyed the day. At our other friend's wedding, most of the toddlers were up until at least 10:30 P.M. dancing the night away; in fact, most of them were the first to hit the dance floor and get the party started! A wedding is a special occasion and a great reason to forgo normal routines and schedules for a day. Kids are also resilient and may surprise you.

Pack extra liquids, snacks, and food: If there is one thing that is cause for a toddler meltdown, it is hunger. Since the wedding was at 4 P.M., I figured we may not be eating until 6 or 7 P.M., which would be close to Sassafras's bed time. I packed her extra snacks and a small sandwich to hold her over until dinner.

Bring a portable high chair/booster: Some venues may actually provide high chairs for small children, but if you want to play it safe, bring a portable chair (or be prepared to seat them on your lap). Unless she is strapped in, Sassafras is unlikely to eat a meal seated anywhere, so I found our portable booster chair to be the best option for us.

Sit near the outside aisle: In the event that your child decides to melt down in the middle of the ceremony, sit near the aisle or in the back to make a quick escape.

Bring a goody bag/toys/lovey/entertainment: Since you are likely to be out for a while, it might be a good idea to bring some extra toys or entertainment for the day. At both weddings Sassafras attended, the bride and groom provided goody bags for all of the children in attendance, which included crayons and coloring sheets, glow-in-the-dark bracelets, candy, and other small toys and goodies. This was such a thoughtful, sweet, and completely unexpected gesture for the guests! But it is also great to be prepared with your own artillery of toys and goodies to help your child make it through a long day.

PRESCHOOL:
A NEW ROUTINE AND LETTING GO

SEPTEMBER 13, 2013

Just a couple months after Sassafras's 2nd birthday, we enrolled her in preschool since we no longer had five-day family care available. While I was pregnant, we had planned all along to enroll her in daycare after my maternity leave and had even signed a couple of waiting lists. I never dreamed my family would be available to care for her when I went back to work, but a combination of unforeseen circumstances (my mother's early retirement, my sister-in-law going to graduate school, and my postpartum depression) and willing family members made this all possible. KK accounts much of Aliya's jovial and happy spirit to the fact that she has had so many loving caregivers watch over her these last two years. I am grateful.

We were able to quickly choose a local childcare center based on the recommendation of a few trustworthy friends whose children attend this school.

Surprisingly enough, no tears were shed by anyone on her first day!

And then came the second day. And every day since. We were all a little traumatized (or maybe just me and Sassafras).

I am told she does not sit in a corner and scream and cry all day. On our second day, I was horrified when she let out a blood-curdling scream, and I had to pry her tiny little fingers off of my shoulders. I felt my heart shatter as I walked as quickly as I could toward the exit door. I waited around the corner for her to stop crying. Five minutes passed before I sent a text message to my husband asking if I was the worst mother ever. He asked, "Why are you still there?" Because I'm a masochist.

We are now in our fourth week of "school" and I can see progress! Though drop-offs are not yet tear-free, I count whimpering and a couple of tears as a small victory. My friends also send me texts and call throughout the morning to let me know they popped in to say hello to my girl and she is doing fine. I have good friends.

Transitioning to daycare/preschool has been an adjustment for all of us. Enter the world of drop-offs, pick-ups, preparing lunches, erratic sleep/naps, and new germs. Only a week and a half passed before Aliya was initiated into the world of germs with her first virus from school, but it wasn't *all* miserable; we lived in our PJs and watched an obscene amount of *Little Einsteins*. Pat pat pat.

The transition from in-home care to daycare is the first of many events in the "letting go" process. Every day I work with college students, and one of the many things we encourage our parents to do at new student orientation is to let go – let their child learn, explore, and engage on their own. I am realizing this is much easier said than done; if I am experiencing emotional turmoil over daycare, I can hardly imagine what it will be like to send my child off to college. Luckily I have the next sixteen years to figure it out! Today, I just need to figure out what to pack for lunch.

OUR ADVENTURES IN CO-SLEEPING (I.E., NO SLEEPING)

SEPTEMBER 25, 2013

Let me just preface this by letting you know we are not co-sleepers. Sassafras slept in our room for a total of two weeks before we put her in the nursery. Before she was born, I had imagined she would be in our room for the first few months, but postpartum insomnia and subsequent anxiety and depression were unexpected parts of this adventure, and I knew early on co-sleeping was not going to work for us.

This is not an opinion piece on sleep training vs. co-sleeping. I am a fan of the "whatever works for you" approach to parenting. So yeah, whatever works for you, do that.

I'm merely here to share my experience and to ask the question, "How do you co-sleep with a kid who has never co-slept?" Based on our experience thus far, the answer would be, **"You don't sleep. Co-sleeping = no-sleeping."**

The only instances in which we have attempted to co-sleep are 1) when Aliya is sick and 2) on vacation. In the case of Number One, what usually happens is we will try to sleep her in our bed, but usually after an hour or two of play, it becomes apparent no sleeping is going to take place. So we do the shuffle back to her room, and in most cases one of us will end up sleeping on her floor. In the case of Number Two, well, this is a recent development. You see, in the earlier part of Aliya's life (before she was able to climb or have an opinion), we could take our trusty travel crib just about any-where and have her sleep peacefully there. Of course, there was always an adjustment period, but by the second night on vacation she would fall asleep much easier than the first.

Something happened when this child turned two, only we didn't realize it until we were already on vacation. We packed our travel crib like we always do when we travel, and she waited until I had set it up before looking me square in the eyes and saying, "No crib." Of course I thought she was jok-ing so I put her in anyway, and we watched in amazement as she swung her legs over the side, hopped out, and shouted this time, "NO CRIB!" So the days of crib imprisonment while traveling were over.

Co-sleeping it was! We all got ready for bed at 8:30 P.M. and turned out the lights by 9 P.M. Only, I think a good two hours passed before anyone fell asleep. Bed mates meant play part-ners of course, so lights out meant dancing on and marching around the bed, singing loudly (sometimes coherent, other times incomprehensible), and sticking fingers up nostrils. Play partners transformed into scary things in the night, since Sassafras woke up every other hour crying any time one of us moved. As someone who has never co-slept, I can only imagine she was thinking, "Are there aliens in my bed?" Negotiations and threats at 11 P.M. turned into begging at 4 A.M.; "If you want to go to the zoo tomorrow, you better go to sleep!" became "PLEASE GO TO SLEEP. I'LL DO ANYTHING. Please, have mercy on us!"

We will all be traveling again next month, and I have no idea how we plan to tackle this issue. Perhaps we will all stay up all night until we are all so tired that we cannot keep our eyes open. Or perhaps I should just resign myself to the fact we may never sleep again on vacation.

FALL FESTIVITIES & 28-MONTH UPDATE

NOVEMBER 8, 2013

Since KK and I both work in education, September and October tend to be hectic months in our household. Now with the holidays fast approaching I am sure we will reach the year's end before we know it!

In early October, we took Aliya to the pumpkin patch near our house where she ran up and down the rows of pumpkins before filling her hands with rocks to take home. She clung onto this little pumpkin for some time, but in the end decided dirt clods and rocks were more worthwhile.

A couple weeks later, we went with friends to a harvest festival at one of the local schools. We dressed her up as a little owl; my main motivation for this costume was that I knew we would be trick-or-treating up in Seattle this year, and I wanted to be able to keep her warm in layers.

Personality and behavior: I must have birthed a ham; she began to smile around the 7-week mark, and has been smiling ever since. She learned how to wink early on, and now she pulls her face in all directions, sings, and dances any time she hears music. She will attempt to command the attention of an entire waiting room, say hello to all of the employees and shoppers at Target, and use her winning personality to get her out of trouble. She is willful and determined, but is able to listen to reason a tad better than she was able to before. She is extremely affectionate and tends to remember people's names after meeting them. I am surrounded by extroverts in my house. We have noticed more and more that her meltdowns tend to be tied to 1) hunger and 2) tiredness. I know other mommies have mentioned this before, and we have noticed that a late meal or nap/bed time are usually the triggers for full-blown tantrums; luckily, we have not experienced too many of these yet! She is the happiest when she is dry, fed, and rested, as most human beings are.

Daycare: We recently transitioned Aliya to a new daycare facility. It took her almost two months to adjust at her first daycare/preschool, and I was worried that she would take another two months for her to feel comfortable at the new center with the new teachers. Luckily, she and her buddy Noelle are in the same class, which has helped tremendously with the transition.

Play: When Sassafras is at home, she often pretend-plays and imitates what she sees at home and at school. She'll often pretend to change her Pooh Bear's diaper, put a blanket over him, and pat and sing him to sleep, and she will pretend to drive and go to work. The other day, she used the spoils from trick-or-treating and brought them to me saying, "Aliya's making cupcakes!" I also watched in amazement as she put on her sunglasses, threw her purse on, Pooh Bear in the stroller, and said, "Mommy, I'm going shopping!"

She loves to go to the park, run, dance, swing, sing, and play. One of the great things about where we live is there are many local neighborhood parks, and the climate in Southern California permits us to go almost every single day. She is an active little girl, and loves to play.

Language: I cannot remember when she started speaking in sentences, but she is trying very hard to communicate with words now and is babbling less. Everything is still in the third person – "Aliya is hungry. Aliya is happy! Aliya is tired." And her favorite question to ask these days is, "Whatcha doin'?"

Potty training: We will be starting potty training this weekend! I have been dreading this since her birth, but I am hoping to be pleasantly surprised. For now I just envision poop and urine all over my house. I will share more on that later.

TRAVEL WITH A TWO-YEAR-OLD: SEATTLE

Last month, we were able to take a short family vacation to the Pacific Northwest – Seattle, Washington. I left home a few days earlier for several work events, and KK was brave enough to fly solo with our two-year-old to meet me there.

Sassafras has now been on a couple of short flights, one at 18 months old and another at 28 months, and we have been able to gather a few traveling tips along the way.

Flying

Choosing a flight time – When we first flew with Sassafras, we thought picking a time during or close to nap time would be the best, since then she could just nap on the entire flight and be rested when we landed. In theory, this would have been great, but we quickly realized our child is over-stimulated by new things/people/experiences, and so she was even more awake. This time we chose early-evening flight times, which worked well on the departure flight (since she had a 3-hour nap that day), but poorly on our return flight (which ended up being delayed 45 minutes and she missed her nap that day). Our flight was only 2.5 hours, and I am scared to attempt anything longer.

Entertainment – iPad, stickers, coloring books/crayons, books – We packed anything and everything we could to provide loads of entertainment. Of course, the only thing of interest was the iPad, which lasted for about 15 minutes.

Other carry-on items – Diapers, wipes, extra outfit(s), pacifier (or lollipop or your boob for take-off and landing), lovey, and plenty of snacks.

Packing

Packing lists will obviously change over time as your child grows and their needs/interests change. In the early days, we felt like we were just short of packing up our entire house (bottles, swaddles, sterilizer, formula, books, toys, travel crib, diapers, wipes, etc.) any time we decided to travel. We soon realized we did not need to pack many (or any) toys since she was more interested in exploring her new environment and playing with cups, remote controls, paper and tissue anyway.

Since she will no longer sleep in a travel crib, I mainly focused on making sure I had enough weather-appropriate clothes for her. We are used to living in a climate that averages 70 degrees year-round, and as I was packing for the trip I realized I had zero winter clothes for Aliya. At home we can get by with leggings, long-sleeve shirts, and a thin jacket in the winter – not so in Seattle! I purchased a couple of essentials (a warmer jacket/parka and boots) for the trip, and we survived! A Southern California native, I am a cold-weather weakling and I am certain I would freeze to death in temperatures below 40 degrees.

Napping/Sleeping

Be flexible – I have always been a schedule-oriented person, and when we are home, I try my best to protect her nap and bed time. For special occasions and when we travel, we are much more flexible with these times. Aliya, who is normally a two to three-hour napper at home and a poor napper elsewhere, surprised us by taking naps in her stroller and car seat on the way from place to place. This was not ideal, but it was the best way to maximize our time out while still making sure she was able to get some rest.

Sleep situation – Earlier in this book I wrote about co-sleeping (i.e., no sleeping) on our last vacation, so you might understand the anxiety I was feeling about our sleep situation on this trip. Co-sleeping has never worked for us, and one of my friends suggested using the sofa bed, which worked beautifully for us. There were a couple nights she wandered into our room half-asleep, and she was able to fall back asleep with us right away. On the other nights, she would sleep on the couch all night, and climb into our bed in the mornings.

Exploring

We have definitely had to change the way we vacation with the addition of a child. As an individual or a couple, you can pack in numerous sights, excursions, places to eat, shopping, etc. and have full days. We decided to stay in Seattle for several days so that we would not feel rushed, and we could enjoy doing a couple of things each day without stretching ourselves too thin.

We spent most of our mornings scrounging for coffee and spending time with friends.

Seattle has a variety of kid-friendly activities, many of which are centralized in the Seattle Center. Seattle Center holds a number of tourist attractions including the Space Needle, Seattle Children's Theatre, Seattle Children's Museum, Pacific Science Museum, and a number of different exhibits, fountains, lawns, and room to run around. We visited Seattle

Center two or three times on our trip, including the Chihuly Exhibit and the Pacific Science Museum, and Aliya loved it there.

Overall, we had a wonderful, eventful trip (not without a visit to Urgent Care to treat Sassafras's allergic reaction to some antibiotics she had been taking prior to the trip) full of sightseeing, food, and time with friends. Traveling with a toddler is always an adventure!

ENTER THE WORLD OF POTTY TRAINING

DECEMBER 2, 2013

I am ecstatic to report – at 28 months, Sassafras is fully potty trained, and she got it the first day!

Potty training is one of those anxiety-inducing things that I have dreaded since having a child. You can put it up there with sleep training and breastfeeding, although now having gone through the potty training process, I can say that (for us) it was much easier than I could have ever dreamed. I have heard and read so many stories about the difficulties in potty training, potty training regression, potty accidents, and resisting the potty, and somewhere in my mind I imagined not one, but all of these things happening in the process. It is no wonder I was not in any kind of rush to get her trained; but I knew one day I would have to bite the bullet and she would have to learn how to pee in a toilet.

About a month before potty training, I took some time to research on Hellobee.com to find what methods and accessories worked for the mamas online. Below are the accessories that were essential for us in our potty training process:

1. Gerber Training Pants
2. Underwear
3. Prince Lionheart WeePOD
4. M&Ms
5. Salty Snacks
6. Fisher-Price Precious Planet Potty
7. Potty Chart
8. Stickers

9. Pull-Ups

10. BabyBJORN Safe Step

I have heard a lot from other moms about the 3-day potty training method, but I was too scared to go cold turkey with the diapers from Day 1. Before we began the potty training process, I decided in my mind what I would try and just see if it worked. As with anything else, I do not think there is a one-size-fits-all, no-fail approach to anything, so I modify methods as I go along and see what works for us. We decided that we would wait to nap-train and night-train once she was older and not so newly potty trained, and our main goal was to get her day-trained.

I purposely chose a three-day weekend to train her since I would not have to take time off work, and I could get in an extra day of training with her. Here is what happened over the course of three days:

DAY 1

Wake up 6:45
Accident 8:40
Accident 9:30
Accident and potty 10:15
Accident and potty 10:20
Accident and potty 10:25
Successful potty 10:30
Lots of sitting on the potty with no pee
Nap and diaper
Successful potty 5:30
Successful potty 7:50
Bed time and diaper

DAY 2

Wake up 7:00
Successful potty 10:30
Successful potty 11:30
Successful potty 12:25
Nap time
Successful potty 6:45
Successful potty 8:25
Bed time and diaper

DAY 3

Wake up 7:15
Successful potty at 8
Successful poop at 9:45
Successful potty 10:37
Successful potty 12:45
Nap and diaper (dry)
Successful potty 3:20
Successful potty 4:45
Successful potty 7:10
Bed time

The first day was obviously the hardest day of training for both of us! Following the advice of other moms, I decided we would have her bare bottom the first day or two, so she would be able to feel the accidents more than if she was wearing anything. This worked amazingly! We quickly learned that she absolutely hated the feeling of accidents, and after the first couple accidents, when she started to go, she would stop in the middle and we would run to the potty. By mid-morning, it seemed that she was beginning to understand the sensation of "having to go."

While it was nice that she hated having accidents, this also created a mini-fear of having more accidents. She parked it on the potty for about 45 minutes, reluctant to travel to any other part of the house. I was slowly accepting my fate and thought we might be living in the bathroom for the next three days. Luckily I was able to lure her out with some lunch.

I put a diaper on her (and still do) for her nap, and by the first day's end she was peeing on the potty! She loved the verbal praise and putting stickers on her potty chart (you can find many free, cute printable charts on Pinterest). We basically broke out into a dance party and high-fives every time she went in the potty. We also rewarded her with M&Ms for each successful potty trip. At bed time we put a diaper on her again, and we made sure to tell her that diapers were only for sleep time now. I figured I still have about a hundred or so left, and instead of giving them all away I might as well put them to good use!

On Day 2, we put underwear on her, which she seemed to think was a huge treat! So much for buying the plain Gerber training pants; she only wanted to wear the thin cotton panties with prints! Go figure.

On Days 2 and 3, she continued to let me know when she needed to go potty and went through the two days without a single accident. On Day 3, we were brave enough to venture out to the park; a much needed break since we had been trapped in the house a full 48 hours!

Post-training Challenges:

Sleep: We will usually try to take Aliya to the potty before nap and bed times, but sometimes she won't go, and will stay awake playing for another hour, and *then* have to go. Even though we put a diaper on her for naps and bed time, now that she is trained she would rather be dry and hates the sensation of going in her diaper. We have noticed this has disrupted her ability to fall asleep just a little bit, and often we have to run upstairs when she yells, "I gotta go potty!" We have the froggy potty upstairs by her room and we use the WeePOD downstairs, so she uses both.

Daycare: Aliya only goes to school three days a week, so this may be why she was having so many accidents at school. I was surprised by how many accidents she was having (about three or four a day), and I figured either she was too embarrassed to tell her teacher she had to go, or too distracted. Her teacher began to catch her in the middle of accidents, and would remind her that pee and poo go in the potty. She progressively had fewer and fewer accidents, and after two weeks she had her first day with zero accidents at school! Let's hope this continues!

Going out: For long drives or trips out, I will usually put her in a Pull-Up for my own sanity. I was afraid to use Pull-Ups because I thought they would be a crutch and it would be too confusing for her, but she still tells me 100% of the time that she has to go, and her Pull-Up is almost always completely dry. If she was just going in her Pull-Ups all the time I might feel differently, but since she seems to get the whole process I do not have a problem using them for now.

All in all, I am so proud of my girl and have no regrets about waiting to train her. Diapers are super convenient – you can change a baby just about anywhere! Now when we are out, I immediately survey my surroundings and make sure I know where the nearest restroom is. And if you are anything like me (and constantly imagine the worst-case scenarios), just remember that your child may very well surprise you, and potty training can be an exciting milestone rather than something to dread. I must say, not having to clean poop diapers anymore is fantastic.

AND BABY MAKES 4

FEBRUARY 22, 2014

We found out I was pregnant the day after Thanksgiving, and for the next three months I went into hiding. I stopped writing altogether, and I sat on pins and needles to reach the end of the first trimester. Maybe it's because I'm Mrs. Doomsday, but the miscarriage with my first pregnancy stole any kind of first trimester excitement for every pregnancy thereafter. It is scary to give your heart to a little person you are not sure you may ever meet, and even still, I know anything can happen between now and August when I hope to meet this little guy. That's right, there is a little penis growing inside of me (though my friend says I should never call it a "little penis" or I may give him a complex some day).

I am as excited as I am scared; I STILL REMEMBER. I wish God had erased my memories of those sleepless nights, but they are still there. One can only hope it won't be as bad the second time around, but at least this time I will be armed with a prescription in one hand and my therapist's number in the other.

Having a boy is another story. The other week I volunteered to serve in the toddler room at church, and what I witnessed was both enlightening and terrifying. The little girls were stacking blocks, reading books, sitting, and playing with toys. The little boys were running around in circles, screaming, smashing shopping carts into the wall, and throwing balls at each other's heads. I used to think mine was a wild child until that day. Now I'm going to have a son, oh boy!

With a new baby on the way, and a boy at that, I feel like I am starting all over again. But I am so looking forward to meeting him and getting to know him. If he's anything like Aliya, then I will really be surrounded by miniature copies of my husband. I'm sure he would just love that.

And so, the adventure continues ...

A LETTER TO MY THREE-YEAR-OLD DAUGHTER

JUNE 26, 2014

So, dear daughter,

It turns out the Terrible Twos weren't entirely terrible after all. Yes, you've grown to be super independent (everything is "I do it by myself!"), but your infectious smiles, your curiosity, your thoughts, wit, humor, and explosive personality have made our lives so much more joyful and colorful.

Whether you like it or not, you are your father's daughter. You look like him. You're loud like him. You can charm a room like he does. Now I'm convinced you didn't sleep well as a newborn because you loved being around people so much. Maybe you knew then you didn't want to miss out.

And as much as you are like Daddy, your affection and love for me melts my heart. Sometimes you want to wear things because I'm wearing them. The other day, you begged me to paint your nails with my lilac polish so you could look "just like Mommy." You reach for me when you're both happy and sad and I love those moments because they remind me that I am yours and you are mine.

You learned so much in the last year. First of all, you learned the use of pronouns, so you've stopped talking in the third person. Your vocabulary exploded, and you still surprise me with the things you know how to say. You graduated from stacking blocks to building things and putting puzzles together. And you learned how to pee and poop in the toilet. You still need to learn how to wipe your own ass though.

You love going to the park, running around, swimming, swinging, singing, dancing, and playing games. You are still the most funny and fun-loving little girl I know, and I'm certain that's not just because you're my daughter. I believe it.

You still have an undying love of noodles. If you could have it your way, you would subsist on a daily diet of mac and cheese. And maybe popsicles (or "popstickles" as you call them).

You love to read. You mostly memorize the lines or content of a story, and then repeat it to your stuffed animal friends. And when you can't remember the storyline, you'll make it up. You do the same with song lyrics, just like your dad. This must be a Kim family trait.

This next year is going to be a big one for you. In the next few weeks, you're going to become a big sister. You tell everyone you're going to be a big sister and that baby brother is in Mommy's tummy. You often give baby brother kisses (by way of my enormous belly) and you say hi to him and that you love him. You bring toys for baby brother and you stuff them under my shirt.

I won't lie – as excited as I am to be meeting your baby brother, I am a little sad for our special time with just you to come to a close. But I am so excited for you to be an older sister, as I already know you're going to be great at it.

You, my dear, continue to amaze me and expand my heart like no other. I can't wait to see the new things you will learn and how you will grow and change this next year.

I am so privileged to be your mommy. I love you so much.

Happy 3rd birthday, baby girl.

Love,
Mommy

HOW I REALLY FEEL ABOUT HAVING A NEWBORN

JUNE 30, 2014

I'm 35 weeks pregnant and will be "full-term" in about two weeks. My actual due date is at the very beginning of August.

How do I feel about meeting baby in August? I am excited and curious to see what this next little person will be like. Will he be anything like me? The first turned out to be a carbon copy of her dad (in both her physical features and her personality). I should have known when she shot out of the womb looking exactly like him. It's like she got everything from him, save for the Y chromosome.

But among the feelings of excitement and curiosity are also a bit of fear and anxiety. You see, I know better this time. I know that entering into motherhood isn't all beautiful and rosy, mixed in with a bit of fatigue. I know that feeling of exhaustion beyond belief (I once asked my cousin, who is a doctor, if I was going to die or lose my senses from sleeping so little because it didn't seem humanly possible for a person to function off of so little sleep for so long). I know what it's like to wonder if I will ever sleep again (usually at 3 in the morning when you know the rest of the world is fast asleep). I know that bonding doesn't always happen immediately (and sometimes, not for a long while), and sometimes it feels like there is a new stranger in your house to whom you have just become a slave. I know that breastfeeding can be a painful journey, and not one that all moms are able to continue through the first year (or in my case, after the first month). I know what postpartum depression feels like, having to make the decision to go on medication, wondering if I would ever stop feeling like a failure or like I could ever get a handle on this new mom thing. I also know that much of my memory of the newborn stage is marred by my postpartum depression, which felt like it lasted forever (when in reality it only lasted a couple months).

On my birthday, which passed a few weeks ago, KK asked me what I wanted in this next year. And I couldn't think of anything else except for wanting to really enjoy my new baby this time around. I know it's hard to enjoy all aspects of the newborn stage, what with the physical recovery from labor, the sleepless nights, the sore, leaky breasts. But I would like to be able to look back on this time with my son and not shudder.

My expectations are different this time around. While I know my experience with PPD doesn't necessarily mean I will go through it again, I also know that it is a very real possibility. And I know I won't have the same first-time mom anxieties again, but sleep deprivation can make any sane person a little mad. I'm really hoping this little guy likes to sleep. A LOT.

For now, we wait with anticipation and a little bit of nerves. All I can hope for is a healthy little baby in August, and pray that I don't lose my mind in the process. Here's to the next five weeks of wondering, waiting, hoping, and longing.

SOMEWHERE IN BETWEEN: 9 MONTHS

JULY 11, 2014

A few days ago I had my 36-week prenatal appointment, and I found out I am 1 centimeter dilated and 50% effaced (which really does not mean much since you could be dilated for a month before you actually go into labor, or dilate from zero to several centimeters overnight). My doctor asked me if I am ready to have this baby. When I paused, she rephrased her question and asked, "Ready to not be pregnant anymore, but not ready to have a newborn, right?"

Exactly.

I have some mixed feelings on having a newborn in my arms. On the one hand, I am very excited and anxious to meet and get to know the little guy, and on the other hand, I know that I very much like to sleep in longer stretches than two hours at a time.

What is different this time than when I was pregnant with Aliya is how I am feeling physically in this last month. While you could categorize my last pregnancy as being a "rough" one (with daily vomiting for four months and having gestational diabetes), I was still feeling pretty energetic up until the day of delivery. Not so, with this pregnancy! I'm more hot, more achy, more irritable, and more uncomfortable than I ever remember being with Aliya. My poor family sits around the living room shrouded in blankets while I run the fans or blast the air conditioner at 10 P.M. I am constantly asking everyone, "Is it HOT, or is it just me?" Apparently, it's just me. I have perfected my pregnant waddle, and I have to tell my husband to "stop walking so fast" because it takes me about an hour to walk from point A to point B. I walk slowly mainly because of all the pressure I've been feeling in my nether regions these days. Yesterday my doctor said, "I can feel the top of his head!" and I thought, "Oh my God, this kid is going to fall out of my vagina." Wouldn't that be nice?

But son, I think you need to cook just a little longer. Take the next few weeks to continue growing and developing in Mommy's tummy, and soon enough, we shall see each other face to face. Also, it would be nice if you gave Daddy and me some time to decide on your name, although your older sister is determined to call you "Boy."

Let the countdown begin!

EPILOGUE

BECOMING A MOTHER OF TWO

It is safe to say I was almost as terrified to have the second as I was to have the first. The first time around I was afraid because I didn't know what to expect. This time, I was afraid because I did.

Postpartum depression did a number on me and I wasn't quite sure how I would handle it a second time. I know I am only five weeks in, but thankfully I haven't sat in the soul-crushing despair and anxiety that I had the last time I had a baby. Let's pray things stay that way.

On the one hand, some things have been easier this time around. Many moms reassured me it would be since you only go through the "first-time mom" experience once. With your second, you have been through it once before; you know they won't likely die if you accidentally snooze an extra half hour, and you're not as neurotic about checking on them every five minutes just to make sure they are still breathing. You're a little easier on yourself and have more realistic expectations about the first few months. If you're not able to continue breastfeeding, you know you won't be feeding them poison or lowering their IQ by giving them formula. You understand newborns aren't always cute, and new moms aren't always in a blissful state; newborns have a tendency to be really annoying, particularly at 4 A.M. when they are wide awake and you haven't slept a full night in weeks.

And then there are the overwhelming feelings – first, the overwhelming feelings of love. When I became pregnant with

KJ, I often wondered how I might love another child as much as I loved Aliya. She had stolen my heart, and I was sure that any other baby would not be nearly as cute, smart, charming, funny, or endearing as my number one girl. I was certain that any future children were doomed to be unattractive and boring in comparison. But little did I know how my heart would expand with love for my little guy. We've had a much shorter relationship than with his sister and we are still getting to know him, but all things considered, he's pretty great.

Then comes the overwhelming exhaustion, an inevitable consequence of being sleep-deprived for weeks and/or months on end. I often wrestle with questions of eternal significance in the middle of the night, like – if men were born with nipples by design, why can't they lactate and share in the joy of breastfeeding? How many hours/nights/weeks can a human being survive without sleep before they die? Because surely, I will combust tomorrow if I don't get some sleep tonight. And what on earth would compel mothers to do this again and again? I swore for the first year of Aliya's life, she was destined to be an only child. And of course, the question all new moms ask – will I ever sleep again?

Of course, I know I will sleep again. I have living proof in my three-year-old. But I don't know *when* I will sleep again, and that day could not come any sooner. For now, I will thank the good Lord for helpful family, thoughtful friends, and strong coffee.

For now, we are all adjusting. We are learning how to care for a newborn alongside a toddler. We are learning how to deal with very fragmented sleep (and how to play musical beds at night when older sister has night wakings). Aliya is learning how to be a big sister. Thankfully, she doesn't blame her brother for turning her world upside-down. She only blames us.

I am looking forward to getting to know our son better and seeing these two interact with one another. And more sleep, of course.

ACKNOWLEDGEMENTS

Many thanks and much love to my family. Kevin, you have always believed in and dreamed big for me, and your constant support has been my fuel. Jean, you are the genius of the family and your words of encouragement have more weight than you think. Thank you also for asking Mom and Dad for a sibling all those years ago; without you, I would literally not be here.

Thanks to friends who have been advocates along the way – Tracy Mo, Angela Chung, Annette Park, Amy Byon, Abe Lim, and Brian Ng.

Thanks to my English teachers – Mr. Marks, Mrs. Ross, and the late Lindon Barrett. You inspired my love for learning, reading, and writing.

And to Rebecca Hanna and Hendre Coetzee – thank you for encouraging me to share my story.

CPSIA information can be obtained at www.ICGtesting.com
Printed in the USA
LVOW10s1508200316

479959LV00017B/854/P